HAL LEONARD
GUITAR METHOD

CLASSICAL GUITAR

TAB EDITION

BY PAUL HENRY

To access audio visit:
www.halleonard.com/mylibrary

Enter Code
3029-0888-2862-0925

ISBN: 978-1-4950-1256-3

HAL•LEONARD®
CORPORATION
7777 W. BLUEMOUND RD. P.O. BOX 13819 MILWAUKEE, WI 53213

In Australia Contact:
Hal Leonard Australia Pty. Ltd.
4 Lentara Court
Cheltenham, Victoria, 3192 Australia
Email: ausadmin@halleonard.com.au

Visit Hal Leonard Online at
www.halleonard.com

CONTENTS

BEFORE YOU BEGIN

ABOUT THIS METHOD

Welcome to the *Hal Leonard Classical Guitar Method*. This book will give you a step-by-step approach to the basic techniques of playing the classical guitar and present in a practical way certain fundamentals, such as music reading and harmony, that any novice guitarist needs to learn. Keep in mind that these beginning stages of your playing are most important, as they lay the groundwork of your future success in music. It is recommended that you carefully practice each section of this book in its presented order, as one technique or concept will lead into the next. Listening to the audio tracks included with this book will give you a clear idea of how each exercise or song should sound, which will in turn help teach your ear to teach your fingers. Finally, while this method will present the essential concepts that a beginning guitarist must have, it is advisable to seek the help of a well-trained, experienced teacher who will be able to guide you through your individual learning situations.

WHAT IS CLASSICAL GUITAR?

Learning to play the classical guitar does not necessarily mean playing "classical" music. It does mean learning to play the guitar in the classical tradition that has been developed for centuries and continues to evolve. As a classical guitar student you will learn to play solo guitar music with melody and accompaniment simultaneously, just as a solo pianist would play. You will learn the techniques to play simple accompaniment parts or more complex music with two, three, or four distinct melodies or parts at the same time, allowing you to play the music of the great master composers, as well as many other styles. It is the approach, not the music, which makes one a classical guitarist. Most exciting about studying the classical guitar is that you are using the methods and techniques that have been refined over the centuries by some of the greatest guitarists who have ever lived.

DO I NEED A CLASSICAL GUITAR?

While you can begin to learn the classical guitar with a steel-string acoustic instrument, a beginner will find the traditional classical guitar easier to play. The nylon strings can be pressed with less effort, and the extra space between the strings gives both hands a little more room to maneuver. Classical guitars are made to play more intricate music. They have a smaller body and are more sensitive to the varieties of color, dynamics, and tone, which you will want to include in your playing.

CLASSICAL GUITAR ANATOMY

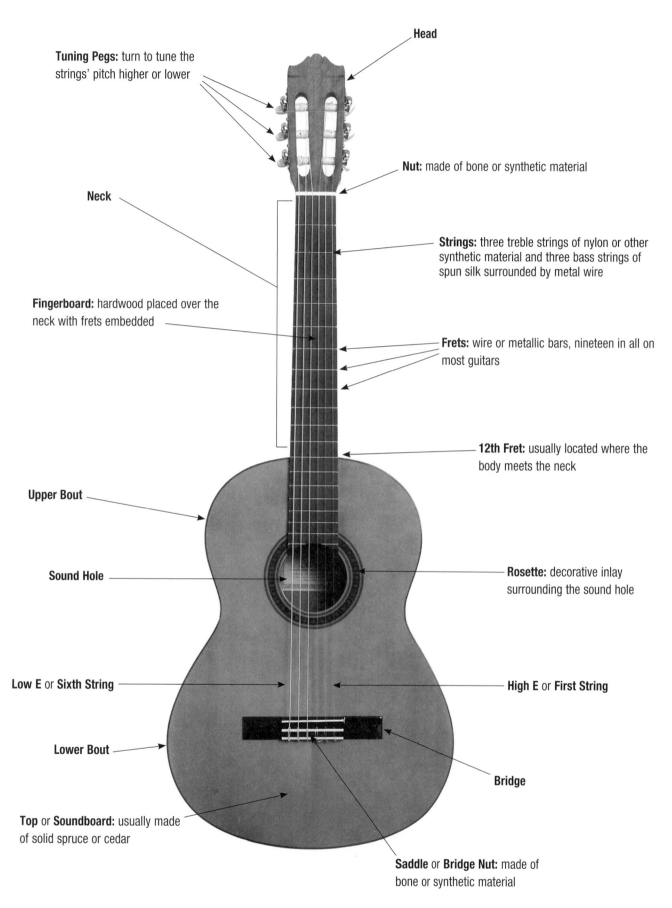

Head

Tuning Pegs: turn to tune the strings' pitch higher or lower

Nut: made of bone or synthetic material

Neck

Strings: three treble strings of nylon or other synthetic material and three bass strings of spun silk surrounded by metal wire

Fingerboard: hardwood placed over the neck with frets embedded

Frets: wire or metallic bars, nineteen in all on most guitars

12th Fret: usually located where the body meets the neck

Upper Bout

Sound Hole

Rosette: decorative inlay surrounding the sound hole

Low E or **Sixth String**

High E or **First String**

Lower Bout

Bridge

Top or **Soundboard:** usually made of solid spruce or cedar

Saddle or **Bridge Nut:** made of bone or synthetic material

SITTING POSITION

The sitting position is very important. It allows your hands to work freely and your guitar to remain stable. Beginning guitarists must always strive for a proper, balanced sitting position. Keep in mind that it is nearly impossible to develop a good technique without it.

You will need either a straight-back chair with no arms or a bench. The seat should be flat and horizontal to the ground. You will also need a footstool that can be adjusted between four and eight inches in height depending on your physique. Instead of a footstool, some guitarists use a cushion or another device which props up the guitar on their left leg; however, for beginning guitarists, it is probably most convenient to work with a footstool.

The guitar leans against the body

The forearm, a little below the elbow, rests on top of the guitar

The guitar's upper bout rests on the left leg

The guitar rests on the inner part of the right thigh

Do not lean back or slouch over the guitar

Sit straight up and forward on the seat of your chair or stool, off the back of the chair

The guitar touches at the chest, but not the lower torso

What to Watch for

- Relaxed shoulders
- The head of the guitar should be about eye level—your footstool will help elevate this to the proper level
- Relaxed left elbow hanging naturally from the neck; rest your right forearm on the guitar allowing the right hand to fall naturally over the sound hole
- Left foot on footstool

This is a lot to remember at first. **The important thing is to be relaxed**. Review the preceding illustrations frequently as you progress with your playing. You may find yourself unknowingly changing some of these basic concepts as time goes by.

Because every person's body is different, every guitarist will have some variation in his or her sitting position. It takes a little thought and patience to find what works best for you.

TUNING

The tension of each string on your guitar needs to be adjusted properly so that they sound at the correct pitch when played. Tuning quickly and accurately is a skill that may take a while to learn. So while you are mastering this skill, consider using a battery-operated electronic tuner. They are a small investment and will save you a lot of time and frustration in the early stages of learning. The electronic tuner will hear each string as you play it and indicate whether the pitch should be raised or lowered. However, it is a good idea to practice your *relative tuning* as described below a little bit every day before you turn to the tuner. This will help develop your ear and your ability to tune without the tuner.

RELATIVE TUNING

With relative tuning you will tune each string in relation to each other. Your guitar will then be in tune with itself, which is fine for playing and practicing, however you will not necessarily be in tune with the universally-accepted musical pitch, which is fixed at A440 (meaning that the A note will vibrate at 440 vibrations per second). So before you start relative tuning, it is a good idea to match at least one string to the universal standard. Do this by tuning your low E to the correct pitch obtained from an electronic tuner, pitch pipe, tuning fork, keyboard, or the audio tuning track which comes with this method. The keyboard notes for all the open strings are illustrated here.

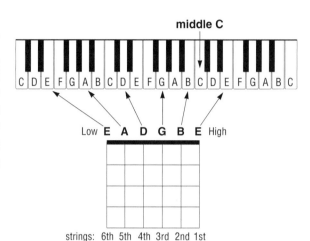

Assuming that your low E string is in tune, follow these steps:

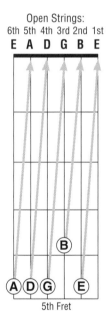

1. Depress the low E string behind the 5th fret as shown in the adjacent diagram. Play and listen to this pitch, which is the note A. Adjust the open A or 5th string higher or lower as needed until it sounds the same (or in unison) with the fretted A on the 6th string.

2. Depress the A string behind the 5th fret as shown. Play and listen to this pitch, which is the note D. Adjust the open D (4th) string higher or lower as needed until it is in unison with the fretted D on the 5th string.

3. Repeat the same process, tuning the open G (3rd) string to match the fretted G on the 4th string, 5th fret.

4. Tuning the B (2nd) string is different from the others. Depress the G (3rd) string at the 4th fret; tune the open B string to this note.

5. Depress the B string at the 5th fret as with the others. This is the note E, to which you tune your open high E (1st) string.

6. Double check. Most guitarists go back and repeat this entire process to make any fine adjustments.

TUNING TIP

When tuning, play the fretted string, listen carefully and memorize the pitch, then position your left hand on the tuning mechanism and play the string that is to be adjusted while you raise or lower its pitch. As your ear becomes more sensitive and your touch more skillful, you will be able to tune more accurately and quickly.

USING THE TUNING TRACK

Another option for tuning is to use the tuning track. Each string, beginning from the sixth (or low E string) to the first string (or high E string) is played on the track. Listen carefully as each string is played twice and adjust your strings to match the pitch.

MUSIC FUNDAMENTALS

Music is really made up of only two basic parts: pitch and time. When reading music notation, all of the basic symbols are there to indicate how high or low a pitch will be and how long it will last. While there are other symbols to indicate other aspects of performing music, the following musical rudiments will allow you to understand the essential elements that you will need to get started and more.

PITCH

Music is written on a *staff* consisting of five lines and four spaces.

At the beginning of every staff there is a *clef*, also called the "G" clef. There are different types of clefs, but guitar music always uses a *treble clef*. The scroll of the clef encircles the note G, which is the second line from the bottom of the staff.

You can remember the names of the lines on the staff with the phrase, "Every Good Boy Does Fine."

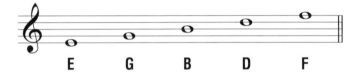

The notes on the spaces in the staff spell the word "FACE."

Notes ascend alphabetically from A to G, then start again, repeating until they are beyond the range we can play (or hear). Some notes are higher or lower than the staff. These are shown by additional line segments called *ledger lines*.

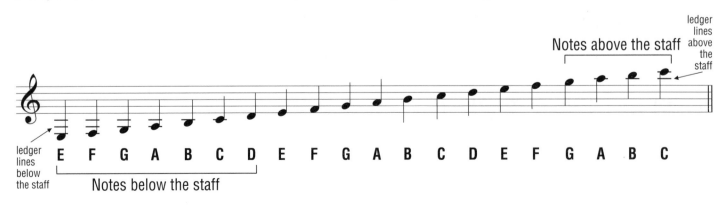

TIME

Bar lines divide the staff into sections called *measures*, or *bars*.

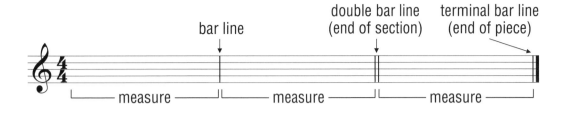

While the pitch of every note is determined by its position on the staff, the duration or time value of every note is determined by the kind of note it is, indicated by the type of notehead (hollow or solid) and the presence of stems and flags. Below are three commonly-used notes and their relative values.

There are times in music when silence is important. *Rests* are symbols that indicate an exact duration of silence. As every note has an exact time duration so does each rest. Here are the rests equal in time value to the notes we've just learned.

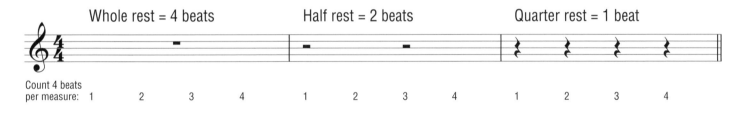

Adding a *flag* to a stem creates an *eighth note*. When counting time, there are usually two eighth notes per beat. Count the second eighth note of each beat with the word "and." When multiple flagged notes appear together, they may use a *beam* instead. An eighth rest occupies the same amount of time.

The set of numbers following the clef on the staff is the *time signature*. The top number tells you how many beats are in each measure. The bottom number tells you which kind of note is equal to one beat.

→ Four beats per measure
→ Quarter note equals one beat

Four-four time is also called "common time," and may be written with a large "C."

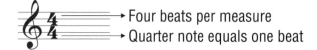

Other Time Signatures:

→ Three beats per measure
→ Quarter note equals one beat

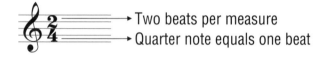

→ Two beats per measure
→ Quarter note equals one beat

TABLATURE

Another form of music notation is called *tablature*. Like standard notation, tablature is written on a staff. Each staff line represents a string on the guitar.

Numbers on the staff graphically represent the fret location of the notes to be played.

1st string, open   4th string, 2nd fret

A vertical line connects the tab staff to the corresponding note staff above. The example below shows the pitches of the open strings in both standard notation and tablature.

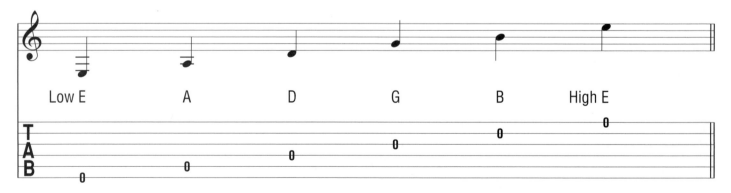

Low E   A   D   G   B   High E

As you start to play the selections in this book you may need to check back here to review these basics.

RIGHT-HAND POSITION

The right hand is responsible for the production of tone, including dynamics, color, and articulation. The correct sitting position is necessary to let the right hand work in a relaxed and controlled manner. Because every guitarist has different hands, every guitarist will develop his or her own exact right-hand placement. The goal is to use relaxed weight and balanced positioning rather than tension to create the force needed to play the strings. This approach will allow a player to develop speed and accuracy.

Fingers of the right hand are designated by the letters *p, i, m,* and *a* as shown here.

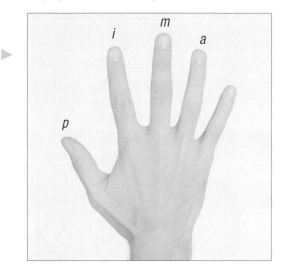

With the right forearm on the front edge of the lower bout, let your hand fall over the strings near the right side of the sound hole. The wrist should fall naturally and will have a slight relaxed arch or curve. The thumb will naturally fall just to the left of the fingers with a relaxed tip.

The wrist will have a gentle arch and should fall naturally allowing the fingers to keep their natural curve while still touching the strings. Fingers should be relaxed and should not feel the need to straighten or reach out for the string.

WHAT IS "RELAXED?"

With your arm dangling at your side, let your right hand go completely limp for a few seconds. Study this feeling in your hand. As your hand is poised over the strings in playing position, try to capture this same feeling.

PLAYING THE STRINGS

FREE STROKE WITH FINGERS

The primary way to play the strings is with the *free stroke*. It is called a free stroke because when the finger executes the stroke it follows through freely without touching or resting on any other string. The finger then returns to its relaxed starting position.

To play the free stroke, place the hand in playing position, keeping the wrist steady and relaxed. Place the finger on the string (begin with the *i* finger on the G string) without straightening the knuckles or reaching. Push in slightly with force from the knuckle. Play or release the string by allowing the fingertip to slide off the string. The finger should follow through naturally toward the palm of the hand, then return to its relaxed position. Practice this same stroke with the *m* finger on the B string and the *a* finger on the E string. When beginning the practice of this movement, place your thumb lightly on the low E string to keep your hand steady and supported. When your hand can remain stable and relaxed on its own, you may find it helpful to remove the thumb.

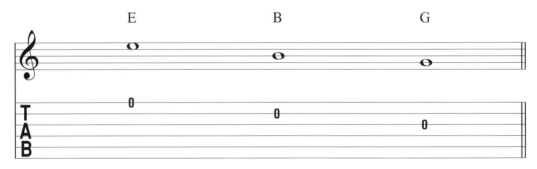

Free Stroke Setup   point of contact   Free Stroke Follow-Through

Take care not to place the fingertip underneath the string. This will cause tension and a snapping sound when the note is played.

NOTES ON THE OPEN TREBLE STRINGS

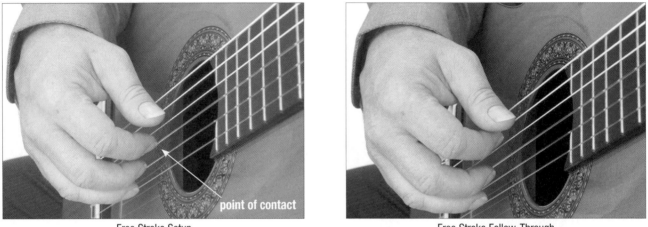

Playing an Open-String Arpeggio on the E, B, and G Strings

This is the first and a very important step in your playing. Before beginning to play the following examples, review the sitting position one more time. Be sure to follow the written right-hand fingering. Keep your right hand stationary and relaxed. Your right thumb should remain relaxed just to the left of the *i* finger. If you find it difficult to keep your right hand stable, try placing your thumb on the low E string.

Arpeggios are chords that are broken up and played one note at a time.

Descending Arpeggio

Ascending Arpeggio

Arpeggio with Quarter- and Half-Note Rhythms

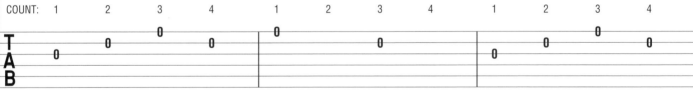

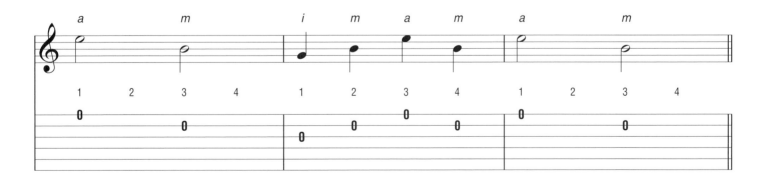

Repeat these basic exercises until your fingers can find the strings consistently.

Playing Repeated Notes with Alternating Fingers

When playing the same string repeatedly, guitarists use two fingers (or sometimes three) and alternate them. Scale passages and melodies are played in this fashion. Practice these short exercises repeatedly until you are able to move from string to string—first with *i* and *m*, then with *m* and *a*.

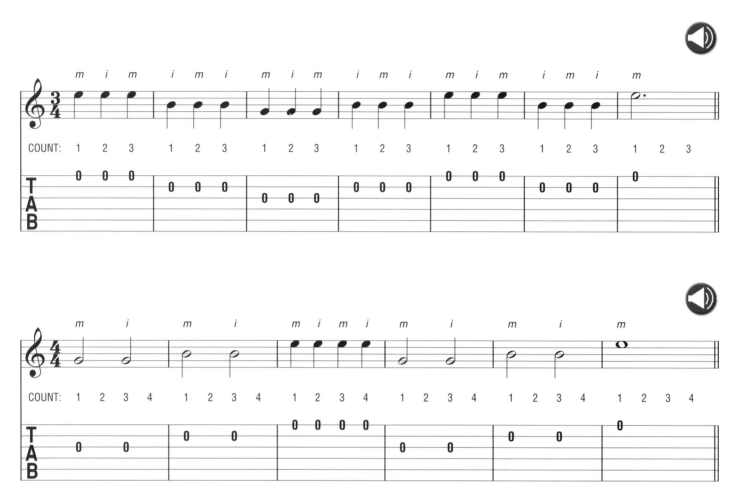

PRACTICE TIP

Do not reach with the fingers to change from string to string. Instead, move your hand and wrist as a unit to poise the fingers in position.

THUMB FREE STROKE

The thumb free stroke is similar to the finger free stroke. Place the thumb tip on the string. Using motion from the joint where your thumb connects to your wrist, play or release the string by allowing the thumb tip to slide off the string. The thumb should follow through naturally, then return to its relaxed position.

As previously mentioned, when beginning the practice of this thumb movement, you may find it helpful to place your fingers (*i, m,* and *a*) lightly on the G, B, and E strings to keep your hand steady and supported. When your hand can remain stable and relaxed on its own, remove the fingers.

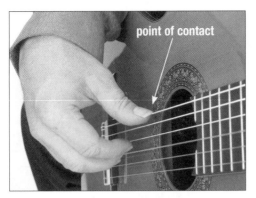

Thumb Free Stroke Setup

Thumb Free Stroke Follow-Through

NOTES ON THE OPEN BASS STRINGS

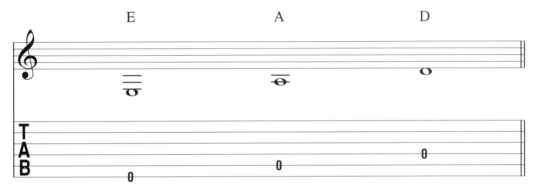

Use *p* for all notes in this example.

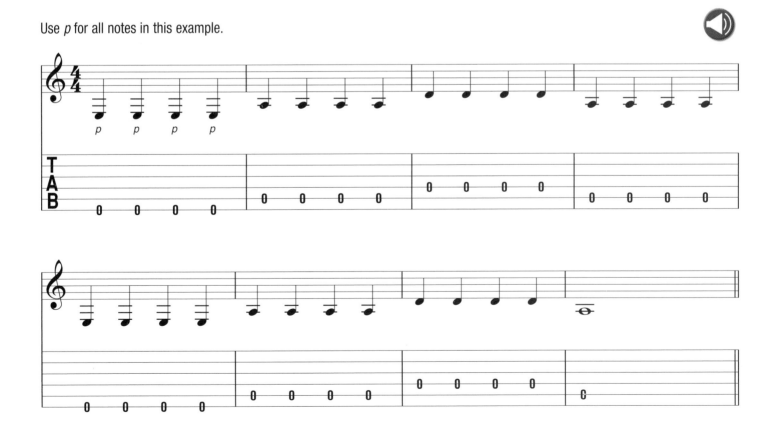

Open-String Arpeggios with "p i m a"

Below are two of the most basic right-hand arpeggio motions followed by a repeated treble example. Practice with a moderate, even tempo until mastered.

Ascending Arpeggio with Bass

Descending Arpeggio

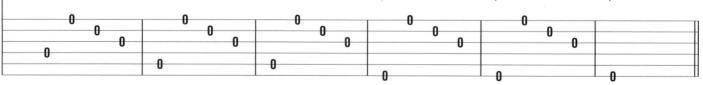

Bass Notes with Repeated Treble

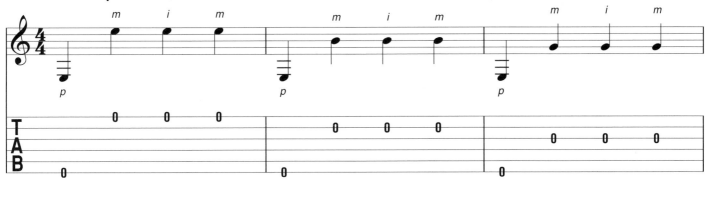

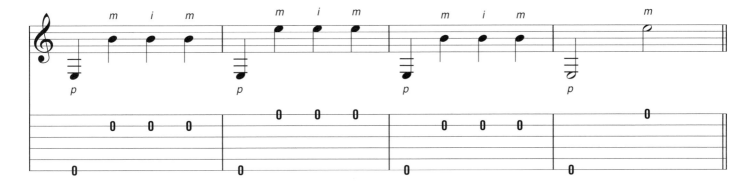

LEFT-HAND POSITION

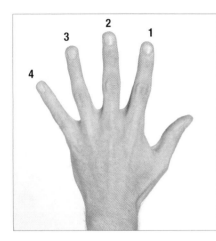

Left-Hand Fingers:

1 - index finger
2 - middle finger
3 - ring finger
4 - fourth finger

The foundation of the left hand is the thumb. It gives the hand its stability and balance. The thumb should lie flat in the middle of the back of the neck, so that the tip does not extend past the edge of the neck on the bass side.

With your proper sitting position, your left arm will hang naturally from the shoulder, not pulling out or squeezing into your body.

Each finger should have a natural curve allowing the fingertip to press the string without straightening the fingers. The palm of the hand should be close to, but not touching, the neck of the guitar.

The thumb should lie naturally on the back of the neck somewhere between the first and second finger.

Press the string close to, but not touching, the fret. Press only hard enough to get a clear sound.

NOTES ON THE FIRST STRING

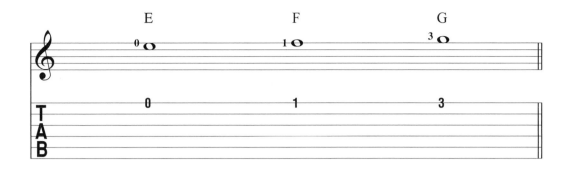

Alternate *i* and *m* fingers. Then try with *m* and *a.* Play slowly and count, holding notes for their full time value. The numbers shown next to the notes in the following examples are suggested left-hand fingerings.

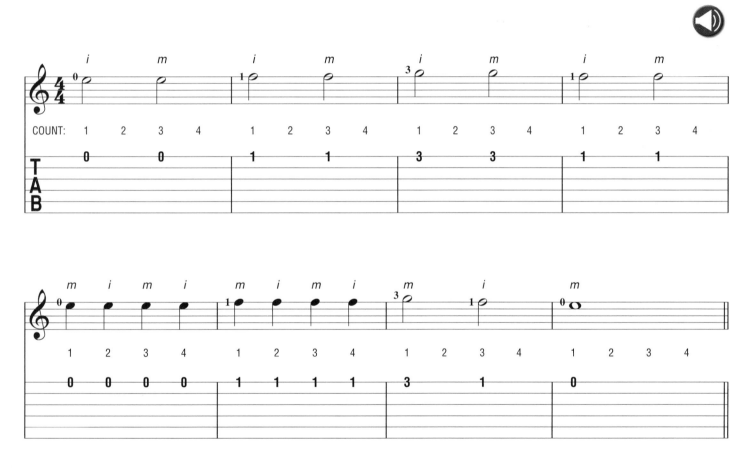

Keep the left-hand fingers hovering close to the notes on the E string so the fingers will find notes with minimal movement.

Alternate *i* and *m*.

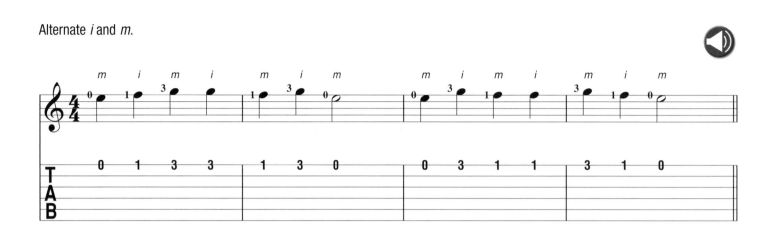

Notes on the First String with Bass Notes

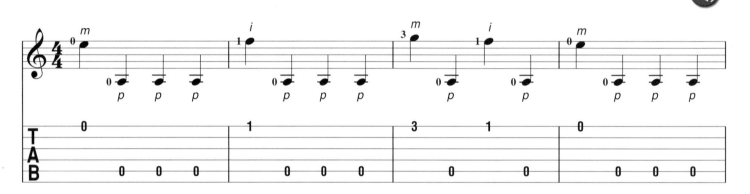

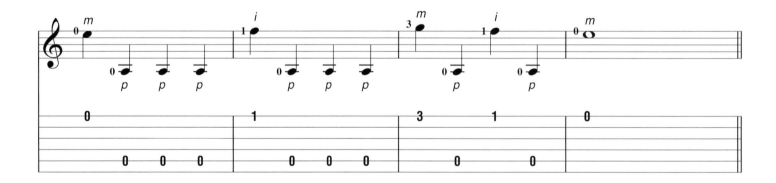

NOTES ON THE SECOND STRING

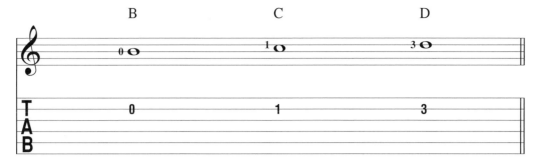

Play notes on the B string; alternate *i* and *m*.

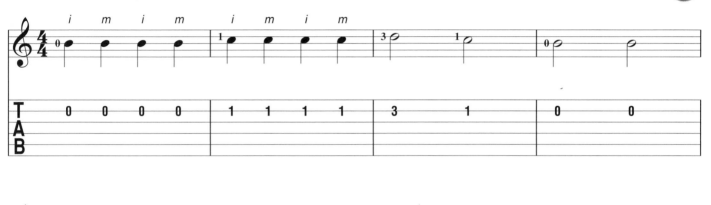

Play notes on the E and B strings. Alternate *i* and *m*.

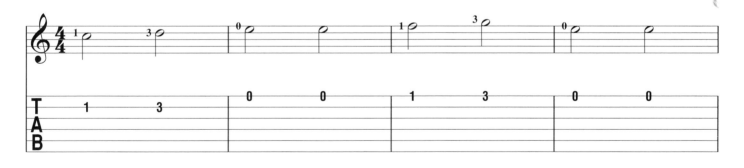

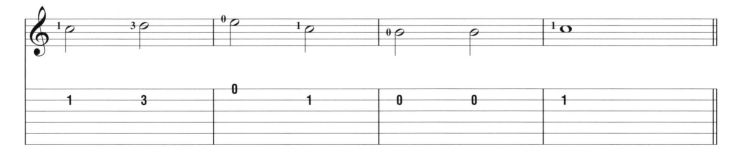

PLAYING RESTS

Stopping the sound to execute rests is often overlooked by beginners; however, it will make your playing clear and precise. One method is to touch the vibrating string lightly with a right-hand finger or thumb. This will stop the string from vibrating. Once the sound has stopped, there is no reason to continue touching the string. If the note is fingered with the left hand, you may also stop the sound by simply lifting the left-hand finger from the string.

Melody on Two Strings with Quarter Rests

This melody has quarter rests. They have the same length as quarter notes (one beat). Stop the sound for one beat.

PLAYING MUSIC IN TWO PARTS

Even though guitarists read music on only one staff, we still can play more than one line of music at the same time. This means you can accompany yourself, which is one of the most impressive qualities of classical guitar technique.

In the examples that follow, practice Part I and Part II separately, then play them together.

Part I

Part II

Here you'll see both parts written together on one staff, as all guitar music is written. Notice that the note stems of the lower voice are pointing downward and the note stems of the upper voice are pointing upwards. This stem direction will help you see the two separate parts, which are said to be written in *divisi* (divided). Later on in the book you will see some music with three-part divisi, accounting for the low, middle, and high "voices."

Study No. 1

Prelude No. 1

PRACTICE TIP

Practice every day! This will help you improve more than practicing for extended periods of time a few days a week.

NOTES ON THE THIRD STRING

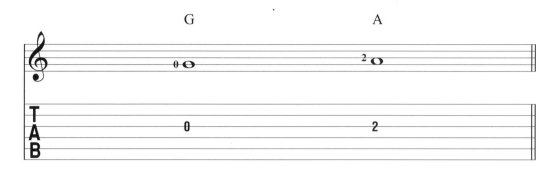

This exercise includes notes on the G, B, and E strings.

TIED NOTES

A *tie* is a curved line used to connect notes of the same pitch. When notes are tied together, they are played as if they are one single note that is the length of all the notes combined. The tie is used to make music easier to read and to extend a note's duration over a bar line.

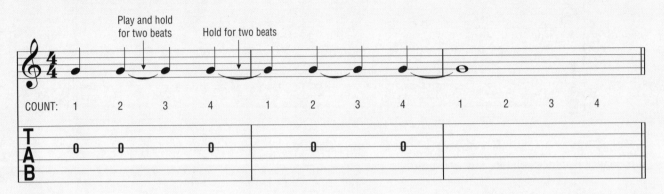

When playing a tied fretted note, be sure to continue to depress the left-hand finger to allow the note to ring for its full duration.

Prelude for Three Strings

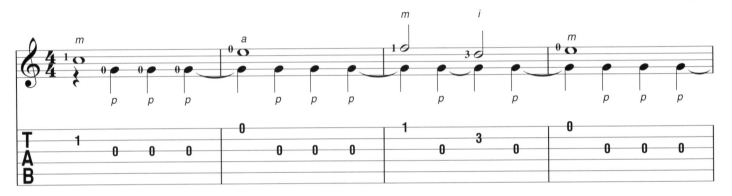

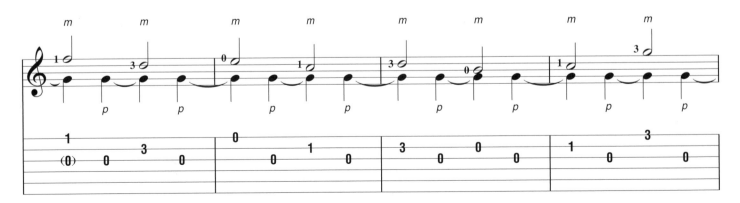

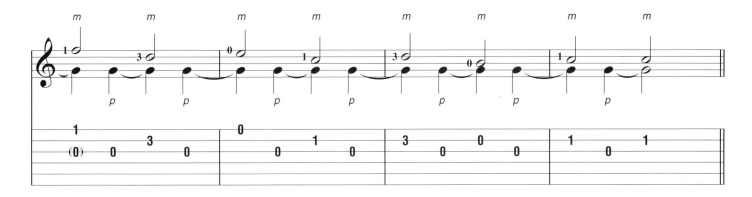

Study No. 2 – Ties

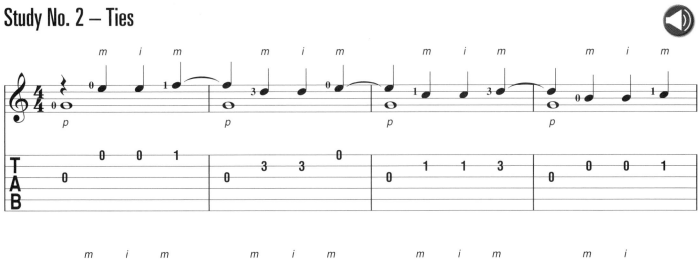

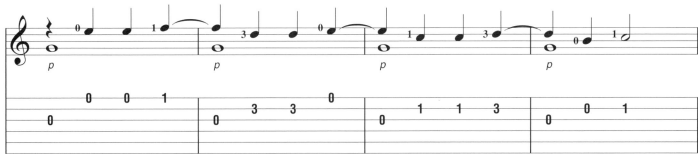

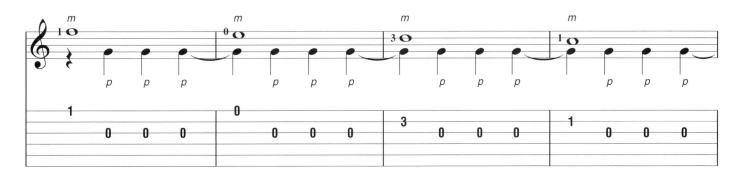

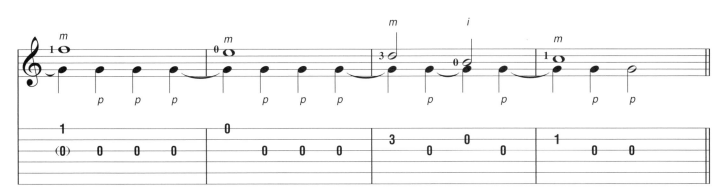

Study No. 3

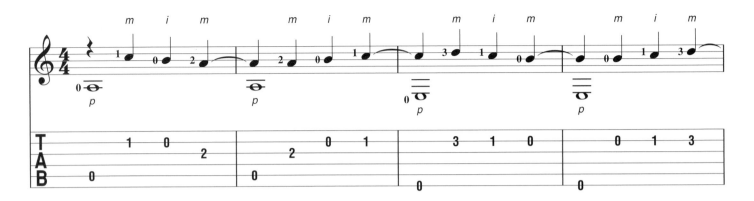

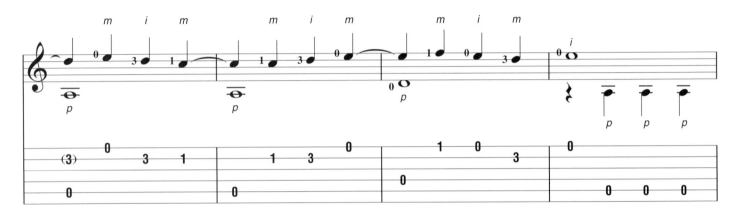

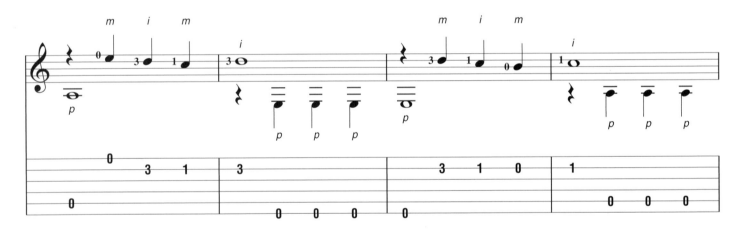

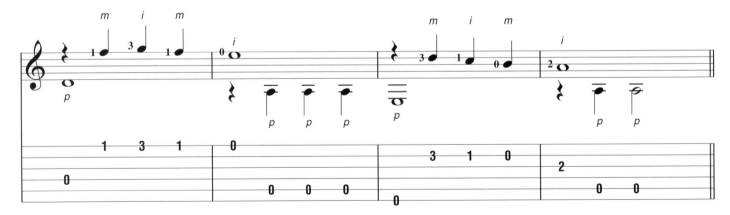

THE DOTTED HALF NOTE

Adding a dot after a notehead means you increase its time value by half of its current value. For example, when adding a dot to a half note, which is two beats in duration, add one (or half of two beats) to equal three beats.

Two Rhythm Studies – Dotted Half Notes

PRACTICE TIP

Make it a habit to practice slowly enough so that you keep mistakes to a minimum. Practicing too fast can actually result in practicing mistakes!

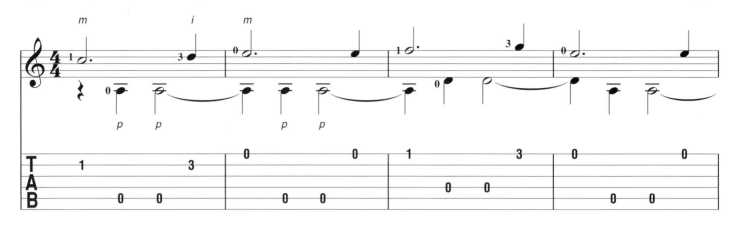

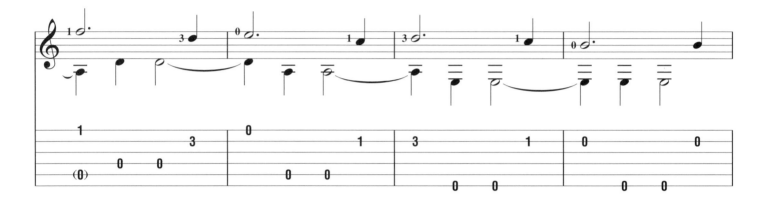

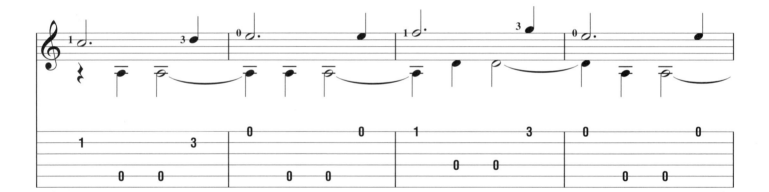

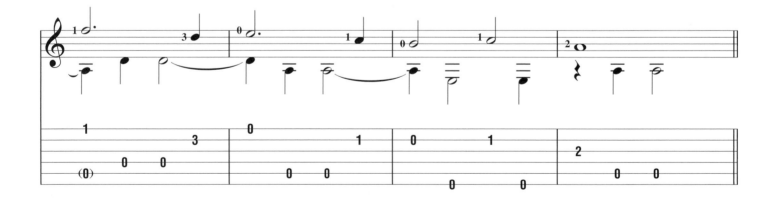

EIGHTH NOTES

To review, eighth notes have a time value of half a beat, so two eighth notes equal one quarter note. Eighth notes are twice as fast as quarter notes and have a single flag at the top of the stem.

Two or more eighth notes may have a beam connecting them instead of flags.

The eighth rest has one flag.

Two Rhythm Exercises — Eighth Notes

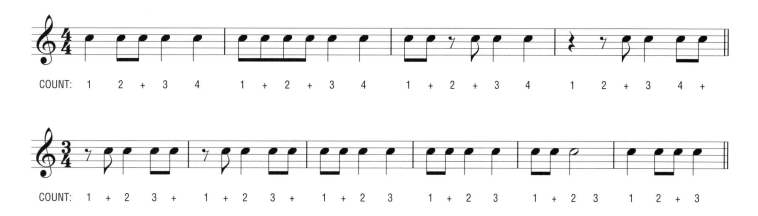

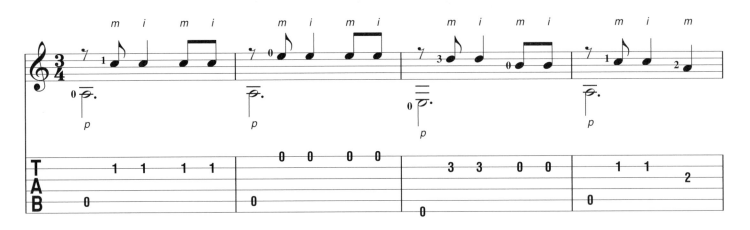

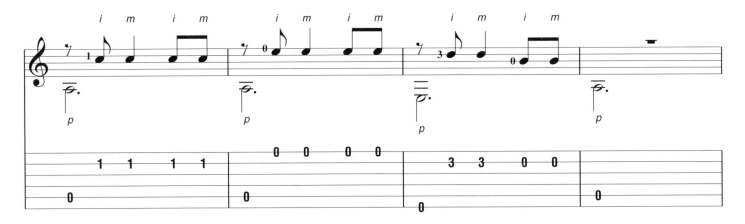

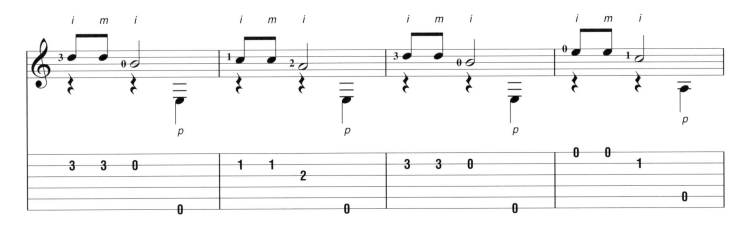

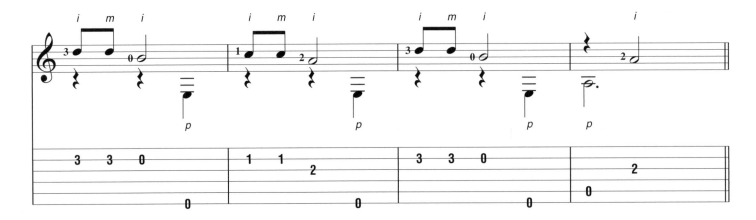

The repeated eighth notes in this piece are on adjacent strings and form an arpeggio. Let them ring throughout the measure.

Study No. 6

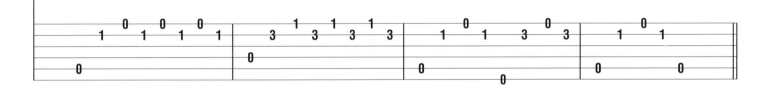

In the next piece the melody is in the bass or low notes, and is played with *p* on the 2nd and 3rd strings. The notes are grouped in pairs of eighth notes connected by beams, but the first note of every pair has a quarter note stem going down, so it functions as both an eighth and a quarter. The right hand should play the rhythm as eighths, but the left hand should hold the quarter notes to allow them to ring for a full beat.

Study No. 7

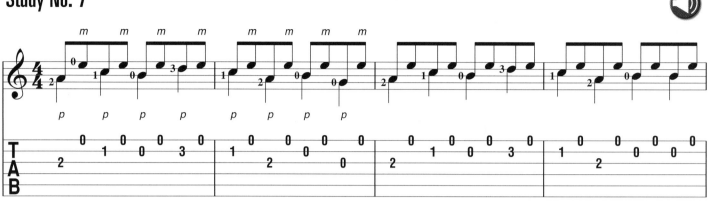

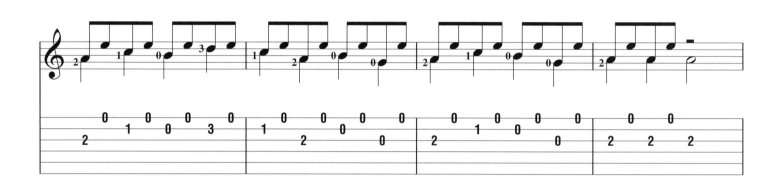

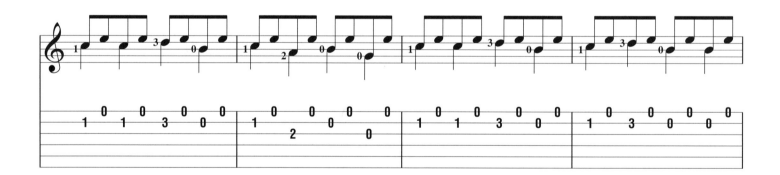

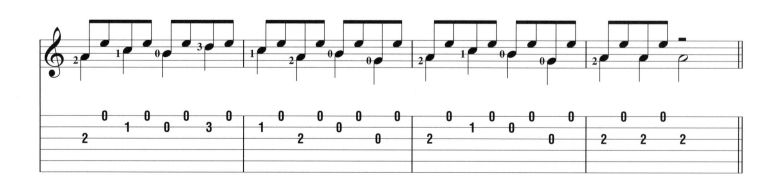

MORE NOTES

ACCIDENTALS

Sharps, flats, and natural signs are called *accidentals*.

♯	Sharp	raises a note by a half step, or one fret.
♭	Flat	lowers the note by a half step, or one fret.
♮	Natural	returns the note to its original pitch.

Accidentals last only one measure and are automatically cancelled out in the following measure.

CHROMATIC SCALE

A *scale* is a sequence of notes arranged in a specific order. A scale composed entirely of half steps is a *chromatic scale*. Since every fret is equal to a half step, you could play a chromatic scale simply by starting on any string and moving up one fret for each note. The scale below is a chromatic scale starting on G and ending on G. Sharps are used when the scale ascends, and flats are used to descend. Practicing these scales will not only help your understanding of the use of sharps and flats, they will also build the dexterity and flexibility of your left-hand fingers. Connect the sound of one note to another by leaving each finger down until you play the next note.

G Chromatic Scale

Did you notice? There is a sharp or a flat between every note except E and F, and B and C.

GROUPING NOTES

Finding one left-hand finger position to play a group of notes will help minimize your finger motion. This will also allow the notes to ring out over each other, creating a satisfying harmonization of notes similar to the use of a sustain pedal on the piano. Look for a series of notes in which each could be found on a different string. The following example first shows the four notes stacked up in chord fashion, grouping the notes you will need to play the following measure. Find the placement of the left-hand fingers of all four notes, then proceed to play them individually as written.

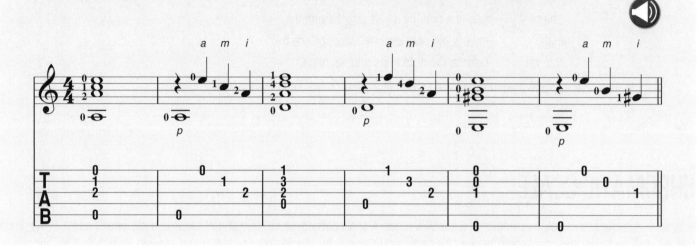

Use the previous note groupings to help you play the following arpeggio study. Don't forget the G# played on the first fret of the G string.

Study No. 8

The following piece requires that you skip over one or two strings as your thumb plays the bass notes. As you do this keep a steady hand and let your thumb do the work of finding the correct string to play.

Prelude No. 3

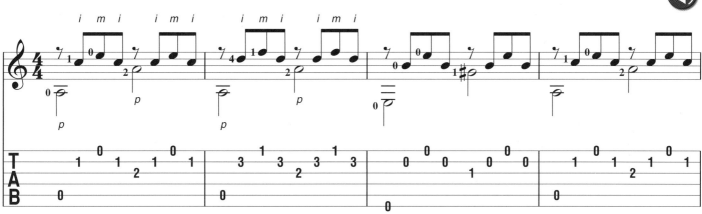

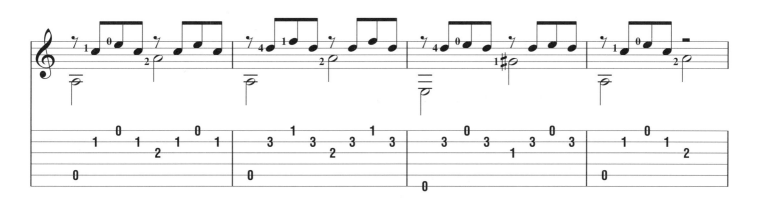

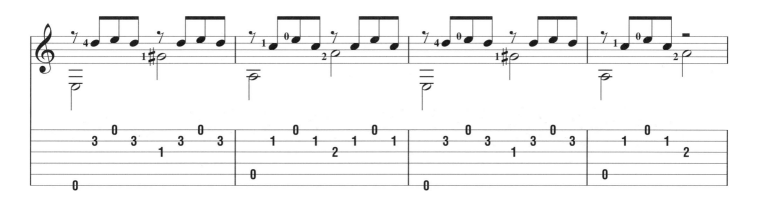

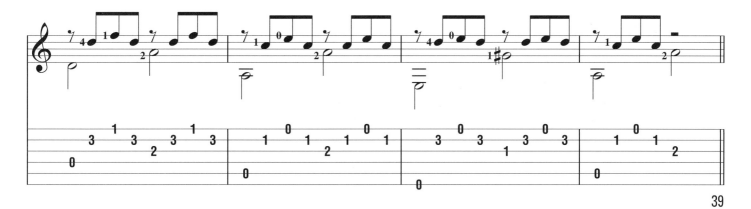

ARTICULATION

Articulation refers to how you play and connect notes on the guitar.

LEGATO

Playing *legato* means that the notes sound connected to each other. This makes your playing sound effortless and fluid. You will have to listen carefully and hold every note for its full duration before playing the next. Try to play so that you don't hear the end of a note—just the beginning of a new one.

Legato Exercise

To start, try playing C and D slowly. Both hands must work together with exact timing to create a legato sound. **Remember, playing legato is much easier if your left-hand fingers are always hovering close to the notes they will play.**

When you feel the two notes are well connected, try to play this scale passage made up of the notes you have learned so far. Use alternating *i* and *m* fingers.

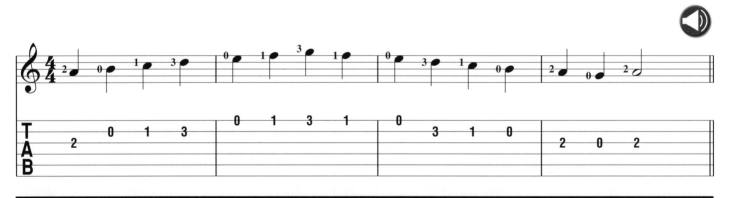

STACCATO

The opposite of legato is *staccato*, which means short, abrupt notes.

ACCENTED NOTES

Accented notes are notes played with a little more volume than the others. The sign for the accent is (>). Accents can be used to bring out melody notes. Notice that the quarter notes with the upward stems make a melody in the following piece. Make sure these notes are played legato and with a little accent. The "*sim.*" (short for *simile*) indicates that you should continue playing the notes in a similar fashion.

Prelude No. 4

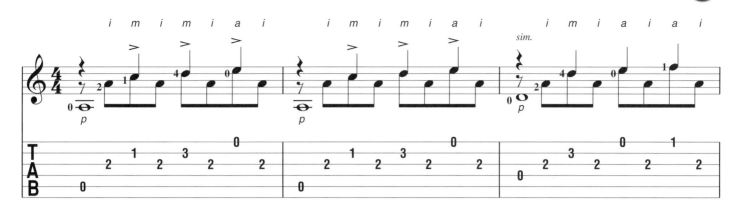

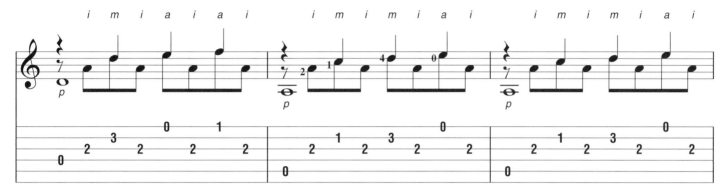

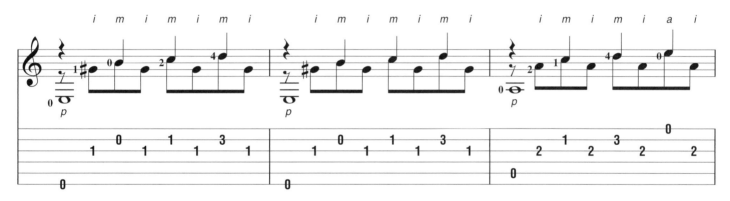

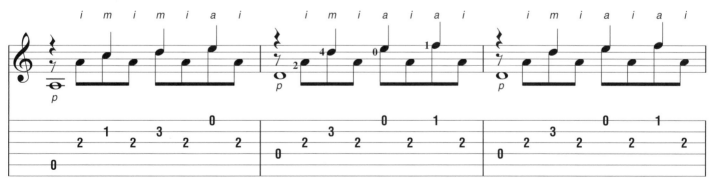

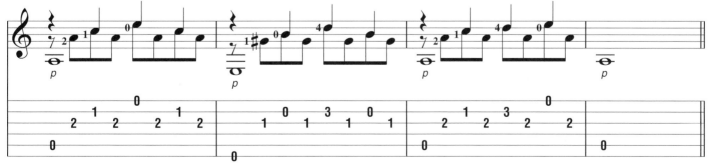

6/8 TIME

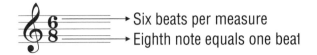

Six beats per measure
Eighth note equals one beat

A dotted quarter note or rest equals three beats in 6/8 time.

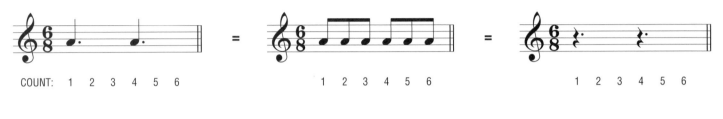

COUNT: 1 2 3 4 5 6   1 2 3 4 5 6   1 2 3 4 5 6

Play or clap the following rhythm.

Rhythm Study — 6/8

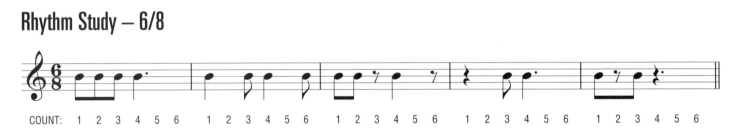

COUNT: 1 2 3 4 5 6   1 2 3 4 5 6   1 2 3 4 5 6   1 2 3 4 5 6   1 2 3 4 5 6

Pieces in 6/8 time are often counted "in two." This is accomplished by feeling a pulse or accent on the first and fourth beats of the measure, giving a feel of two groups of three. When the beat is equal to a dotted note like this, it's referred to as a *compound meter*.

This piece uses the *pimami* arpeggio pattern. It is a good piece to memorize. Concentrate on keeping a steady rhythm throughout. Try to give it a feel of two beats per measure by accenting beats 1 and 4.

Study No. 9

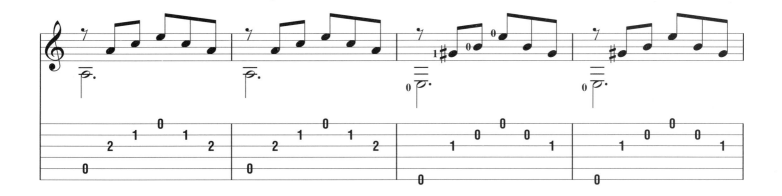

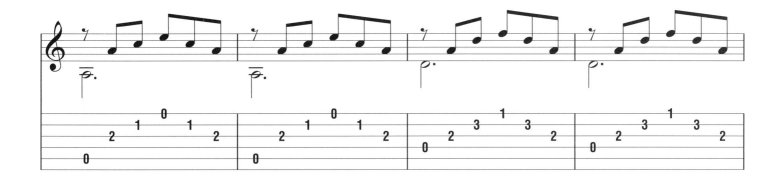

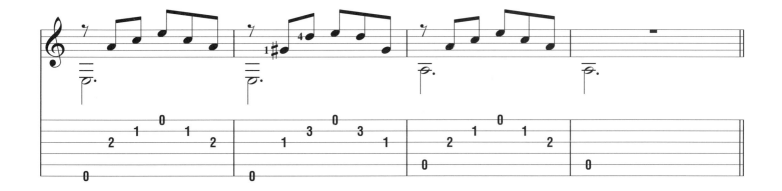

This piece uses a stepwise or scale-like melody. Use *i* and *m* in alternation for the melody.

Prelude No. 5

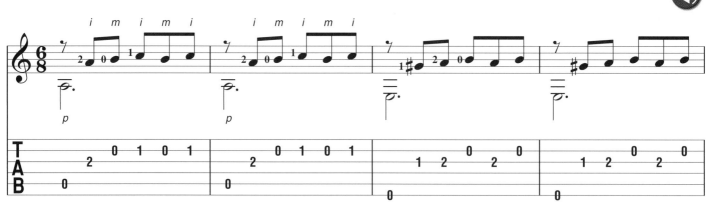

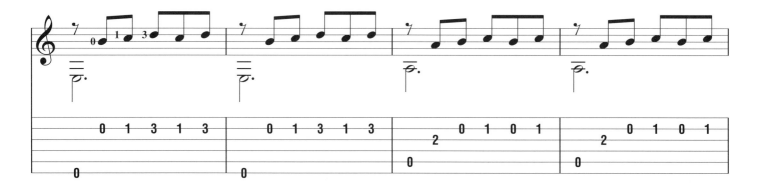

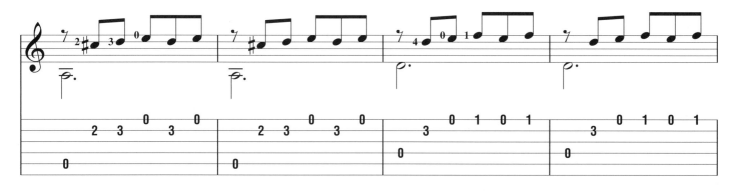

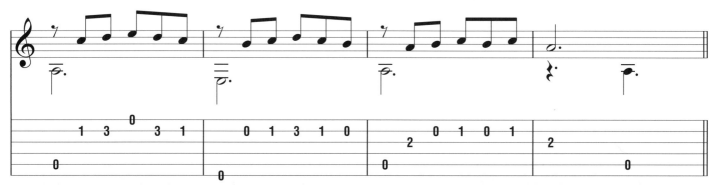

KEY SIGNATURES

When certain notes in a piece are always played with a sharp or a flat it is more practical to indicate this at the beginning of the staff rather than using accidentals for every altered note. The notes that will always be played with sharps or flats will be indicated just to the right of the G clef. This is a *key signature*. Check the beginning of every piece to see which notes will be played with sharps or flats.

The next piece is in the key of D major. It has two sharped notes (F♯ and C♯). Play them as sharps throughout the piece.

Prelude No. 6 in D

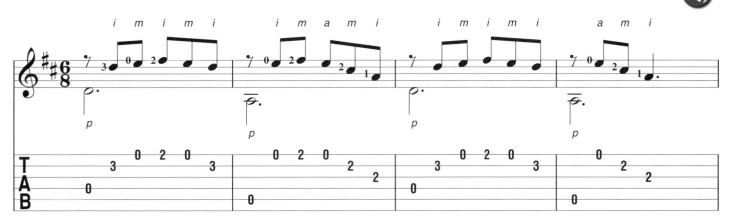

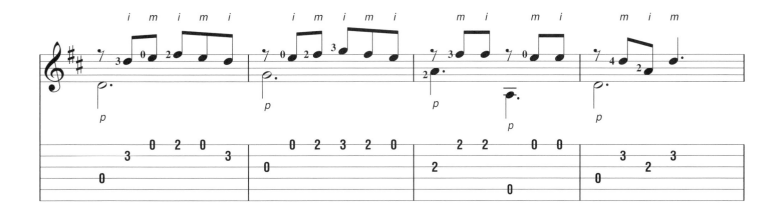

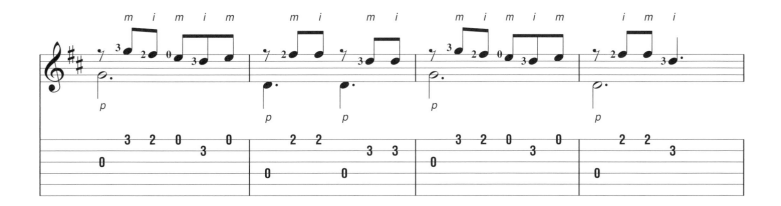

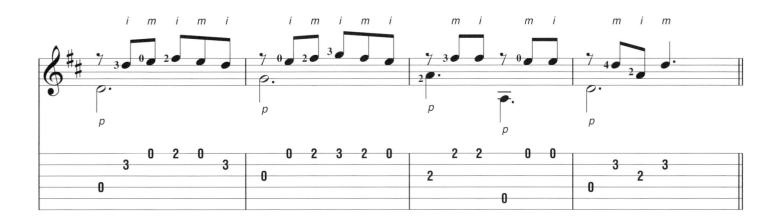

Etude is another word for study. This etude is challenging. It contains many of the concepts that have been covered thus far in this book, including accidentals, changing note values, scale passages, and legato playing. Take care to use correct fingering and proceed slowly and carefully at first.

Remember, once a sharp or flat is placed in front of a note it remains in effect for the full measure unless cancelled out by a natural sign.

Study No. 10

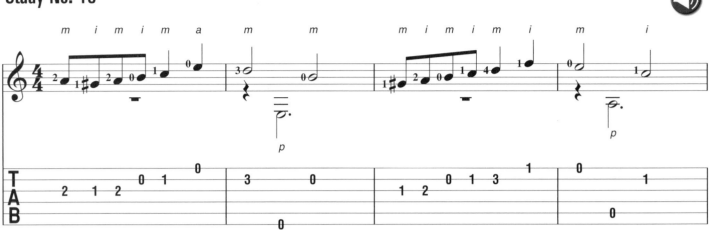

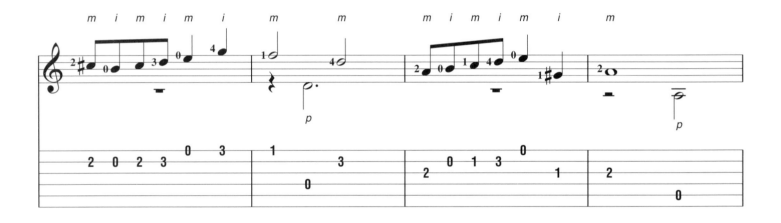

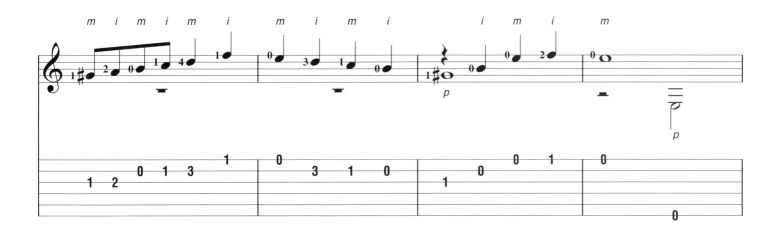

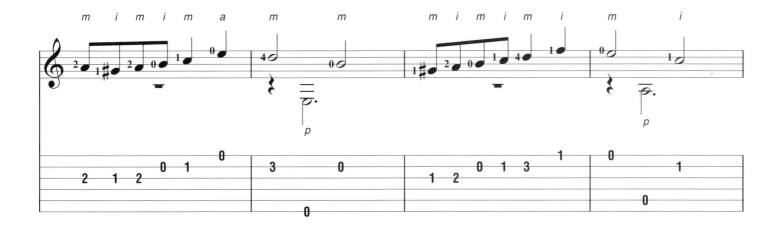

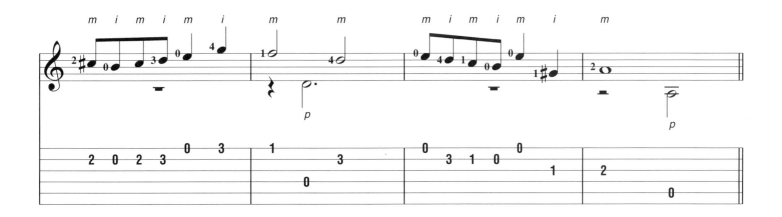

NOTES ON THE FOURTH STRING

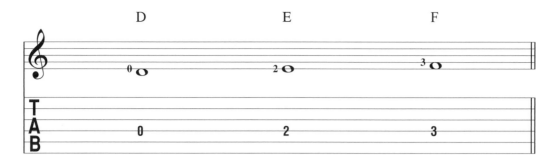

D   E   F

Use *p* for all notes in this example.

THEME IN D MINOR

Don't forget! In this next example, the key signature shows that every B note is flat. Find B♭ on the third fret of the third string.

VARIATION ON A THEME IN D MINOR

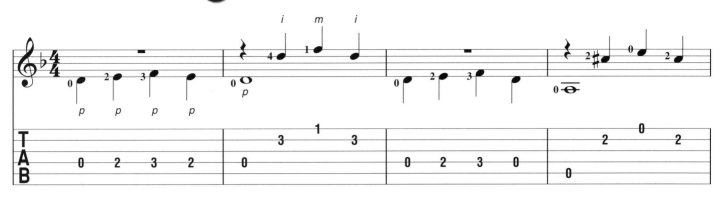

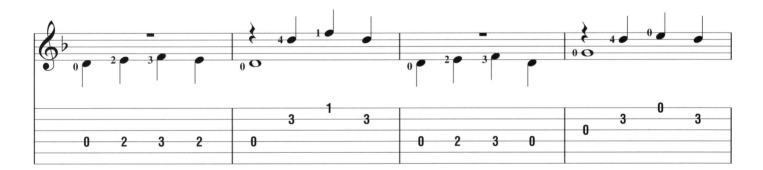

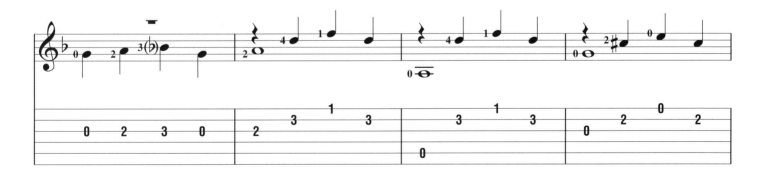

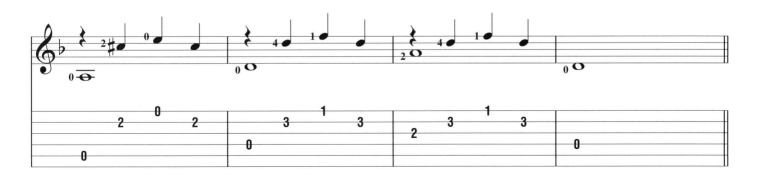

PLAYING TWO NOTES TOGETHER WITH I AND M

When playing two notes with *i* and *m* use the same motion as with one finger. Take care to place the fingertips of both fingers at the same place on each string so that the notes can be played exactly together. Follow through toward your palm.

Study No. 11

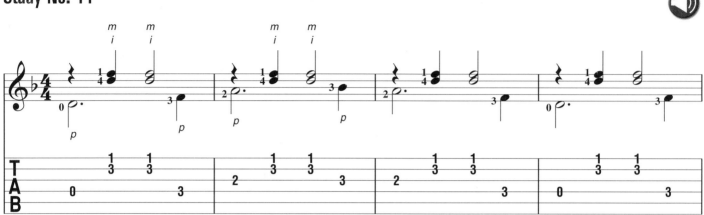

NOTES ON THE FIFTH STRING

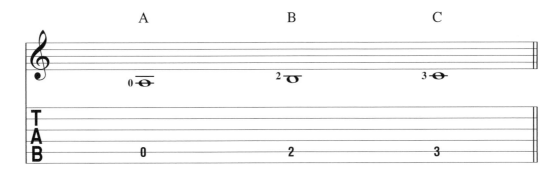

Use *p* for all notes.

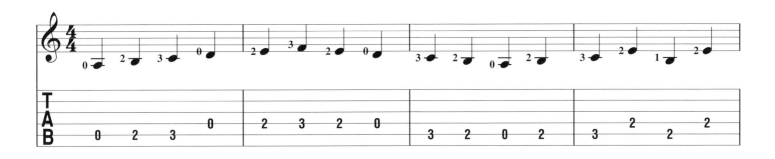

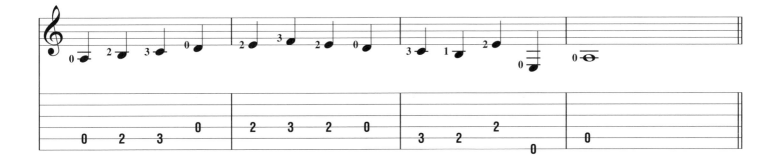

In the next example, use *p* for the bass melody and alternate *m* and *i* to play the repeated E notes. Keep the bass melody legato.

Study No. 12

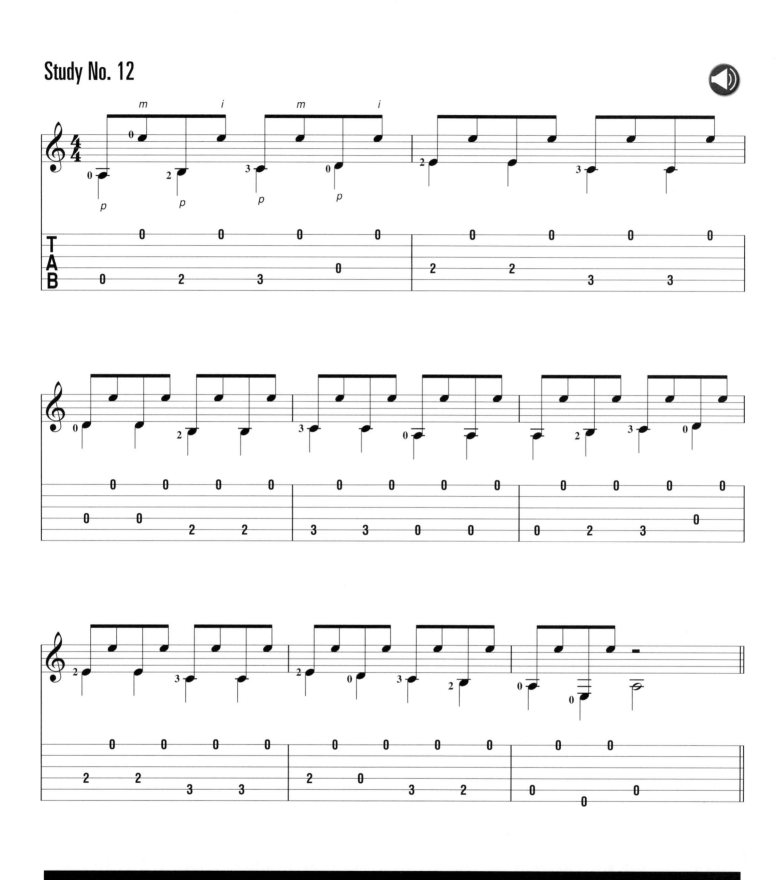

PRACTICE TIP

Try to project a full tone whenever you practice.

NOTES ON THE SIXTH STRING

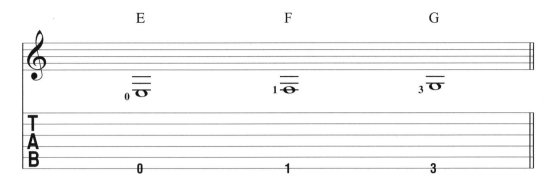

Use *p* for all notes.

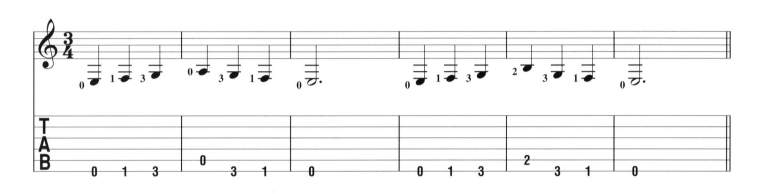

FANTASIA

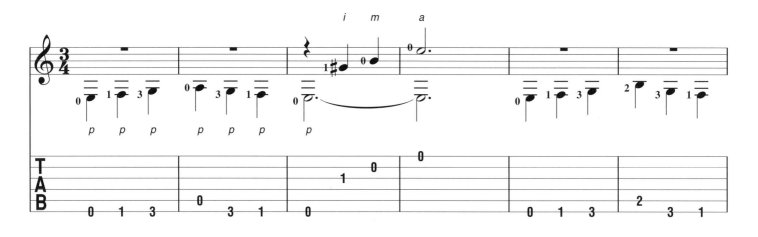

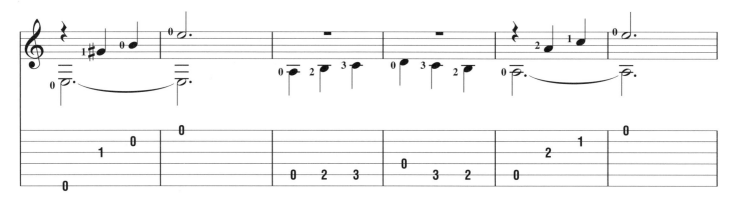

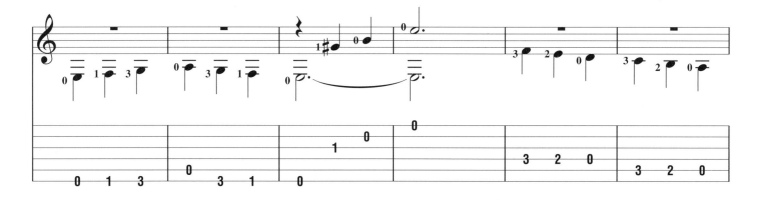

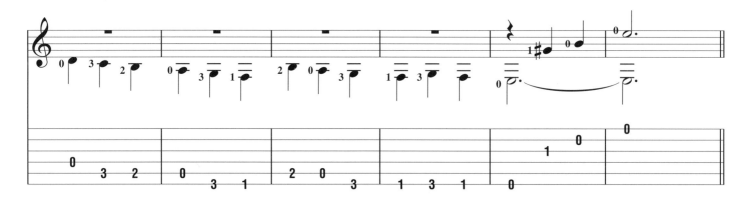

SCALES

A *scale* is a series of notes that ascend in a specific stepwise pattern. In order to understand how a scale is built you must know the *intervals* (distances between notes) which separate the notes. In a major scale each note is separated from the next by an interval of a whole step or a half step. On the guitar, a whole step is equal to two frets, and a half step is equal to one fret.

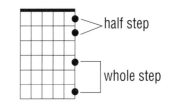

The most common scale is the major scale. Every major scale will have the following pattern of whole steps and half steps separating the notes.

whole—whole—half—whole—whole—whole—half

Below is the C major scale. It starts and ends on C.

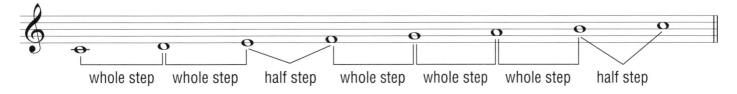

The same pattern of whole steps and half steps starting on G will produce the G major scale.

A natural minor scale has a different pattern as seen below in the A minor natural scale.

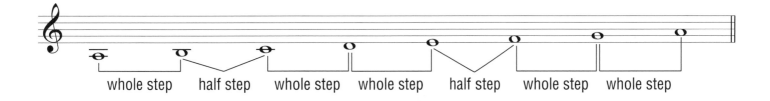

Scales are the foundation of music. Understanding them is fundamental in your musical education.

The next exercise is built from the notes of the *C major scale* and from all the notes covered in this method to this point. Practice this scale a few times every day. Use *i* and *m,* then *m* and *a.* Keep a moderate and even tempo and play with a legato sound. This is a good scale to play from memory. Playing from memory allows you to concentrate on the quality of your tone and technique.

Scale Exercise

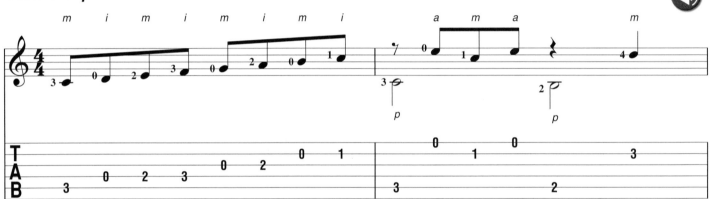

Scale Study

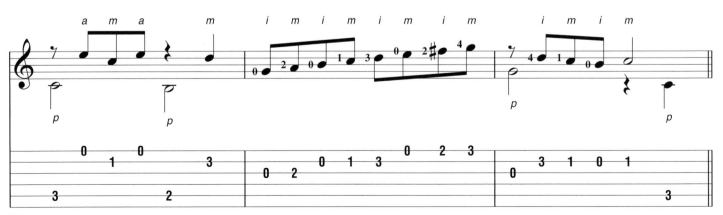

CHORDS

Chords are three or more notes played together.

PLAYING THREE NOTES TOGETHER WITH I, M, AND A

When playing three notes together with *ima* use the same motion as with one finger. Take care to place the tips of all fingers on the strings at the same place so that the notes can be played exactly together. Let the fingers follow through toward your palm and relax them when your thumb plays.

Study No. 13

PLAYING NOTES TOGETHER WITH P AND A

In the Romance below the *a* finger is played together with the thumb. Keep your right hand still and relaxed as usual. Use the same independent motion as if the notes were played separately, while carefully following the right-hand fingering.

ROMANCE

In the next study place your thumb and fingers on the strings at the same time; when playing the strings, make sure all three strings sound simultaneously.

Practice with *pim* and then with *pma*.

Study No. 14

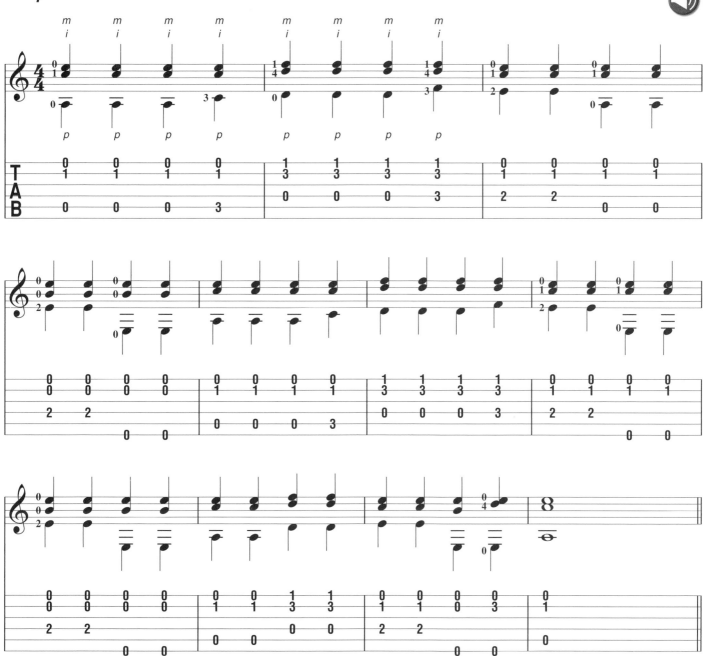

In the following Chorale, *ima* are played together with the thumb, for a total of four notes, using the same technique as previously described for three-note chords. The active melody starts with the repeated bass notes, then moves to the high notes. The challenge is to keep the melody legato, wherever it appears, while playing the chords with *pima*.

D.C. AL FINE

D.C. al fine is an abbreviation for "da capo al fine," which translates to "from the head to the end." This is an instruction to return to the beginning and play to the *fine* or end.

CHORALE

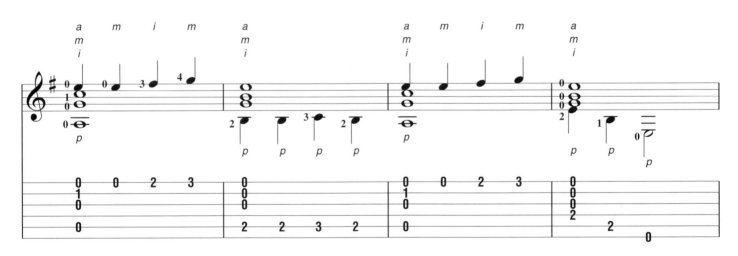

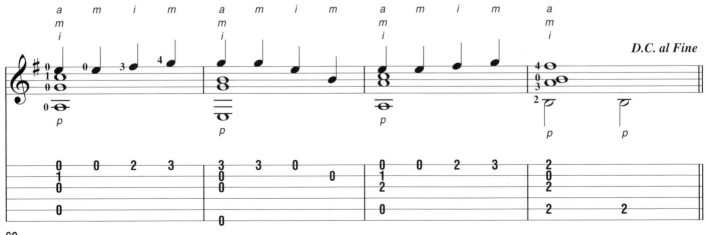

PIECES

MEMORIZATION

Nearly all musicians who wish to give their best performance will play from memory. At this point in your playing you have learned all the notes in the first position and have learned to play pieces with a variety of techniques. Now is a good time to begin memorizing a few pieces. This will greatly improve your playing and give you more confidence. Concentrate not only on remembering the notes but also on your technique, efficiency of motion, and keeping a steady tempo. Before you start to memorize, read through the piece a few times, making sure of the notes and correct fingering. Memorize a few measures at a time, checking with the music as needed. Isolate and work extra hard at the tricky spots. Repetition is what solidifies both your muscle memory and your cognitive memory. After a few days you will find that your playing will become more fluid and effortless. Most importantly, keep in mind that you will get good at what you practice, so practice the correct things.

Ferdinando Carulli (1770–1841)

Carulli was a composer and famous guitarist of his day. Born in Naples, Italy, he played cello before turning to the guitar as his main instrument. He composed hundreds of works for guitar and was also an active teacher and performer. He moved to Paris in 1808, where he remained until his death in 1841.

Following are two pieces by Carulli. The first piece is in 3/8 time. This means you count three beats in each measure, and the eighth note is equal to one beat.

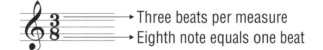

Three beats per measure
Eighth note equals one beat

REPEAT SIGN

In some pieces you will find a signle left-facing repeat sign. This sign instructs you to replay all of the music you have played from the beginning.

When you see the two repeat signs—a beginning and an ending repeat sign—it means that you repeat the measurements in between these two signs.

ALLEGRO

Ferdinando Carulli

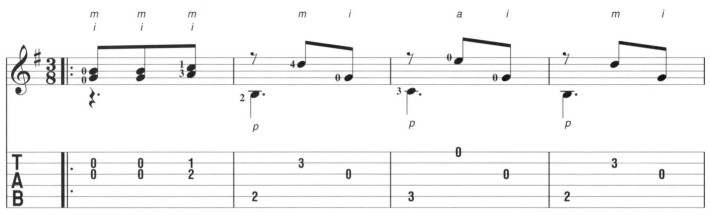

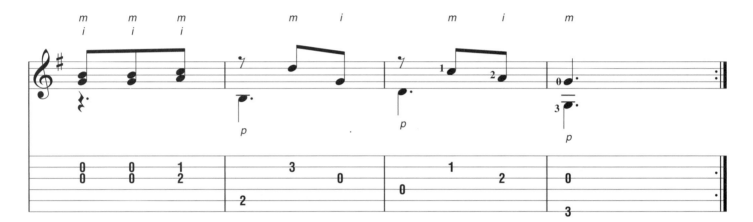

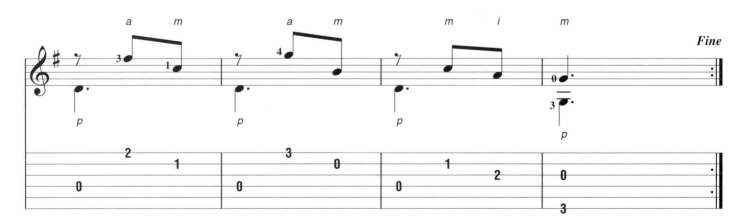

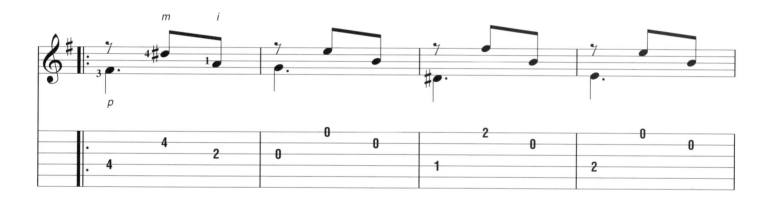

2nd time, D.C. al Fine
(no repeats)

WALTZ

Ferdinando Carulli

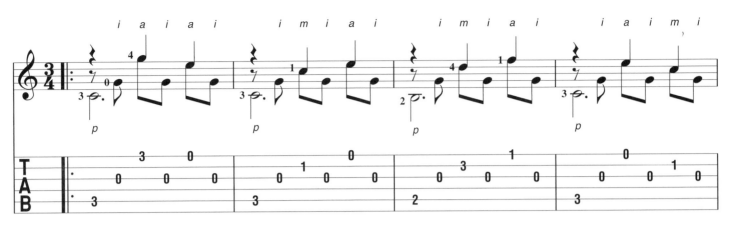

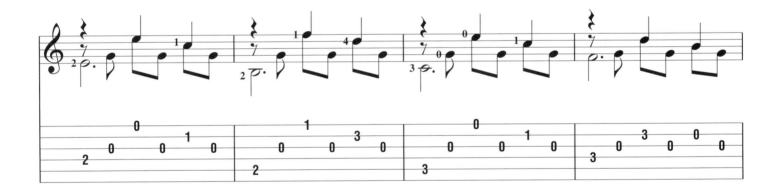

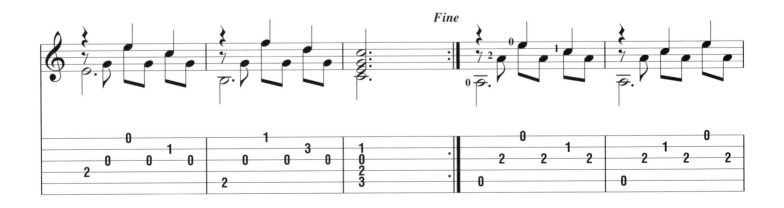

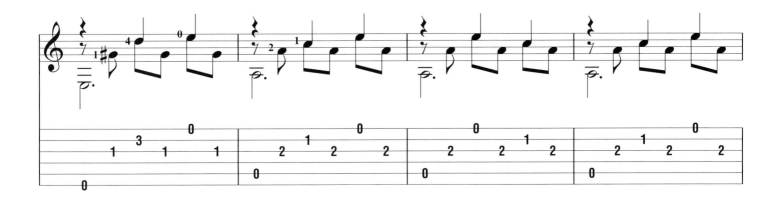

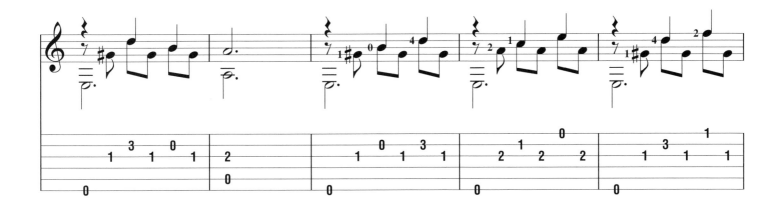

D.C. al Fine
(no repeats)

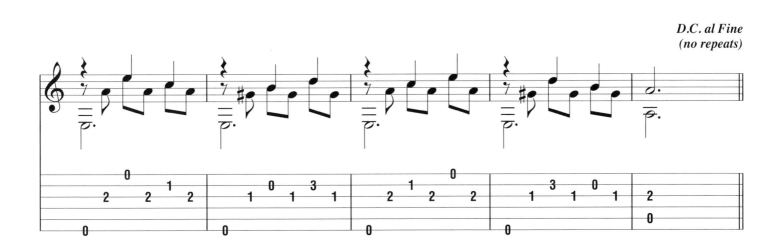

Matteo Carcassi (1792–1853)

Matteo Carcassi was one of the leading guitarist-composers of the nineteenth century, born in Florence in 1792. He was a master guitarist, touring throughout Europe, performing in the most prestigious venues, including an extremely successful series of concerts in London that gained him great fame both as a performing artist and as a teacher. Carcassi wrote a method for guitar (Op. 59). His most famous works are collected in his *25 Etudes Op. 60* that still are very popular among guitarists. Retiring from performing around 1840, he later died in Paris in 1853.

 **ANDANTINO**

Matteo Carcassi

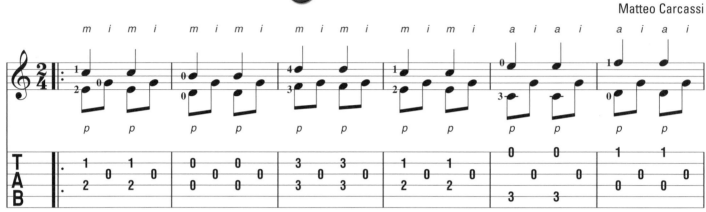

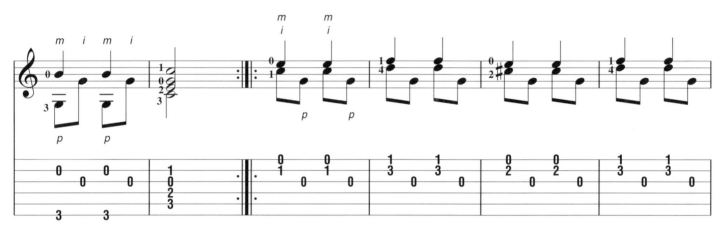

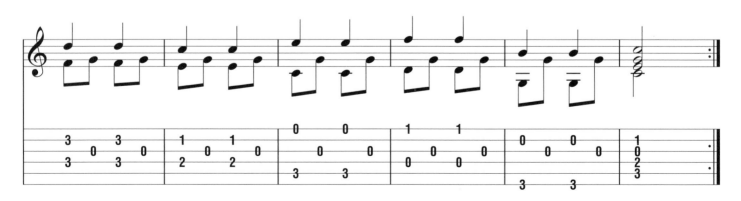

PICKUP NOTES

Sometimes the beginning of a piece will start with an incomplete measure, where there are not enough notes or rests in the measure to equal the top number in the time signature. The note or notes in this first measure are called *pickup notes*. Whatever number of beats is missing in the first measure will be "picked up," usually at the end of the song in the last measure, which will also be an incomplete measure.

Robert Schumann (1810–1856)

Robert Schumann was born in Zwickau, Germany on June 8, 1810, as the son of a book-seller. He was a pianist, composer, critic, and music journalist. Beginning at the age of seven to compose small pieces, he went on to compose music for piano, orchestra, voice, and string ensembles.

The following Andante by Schumann contains a pickup; it starts on the third beat of a 3/4 measure. The last measure of the piece contains only two beats.

ANDANTE

Robert Schumann

Francesco Bathioli (?–1830?)

Little is known about Francesco Bathioli. Most likely born in Italy, he made his way to Vienna as many musicians did during this period. He published 12 compositions for guitar including a concerto for guitar and string quartet. He lived the last few years of his life in Venice, Italy.

HUNGARIAN AIR

Francesco Bathioli

MORE CHORDS

Classical guitarists traditionally tend to read notes rather than play from a chord chart, but if you already play a few chords you may have noticed some of the notes you have been playing are forming some chords. Knowing these chords may help you remember a group of notes in the piece. There are several commonly-used chords and a few essential chord progressions that every guitarist should be comfortable with. As you improve your classical guitar playing you will see that many of the pieces you play are based on chords, so knowing them will give you helpful insight to the music. Improvising with chords can also be fun and creative. Try using different finger or strumming patterns with the chord progressions below. While chords are most useful to accompany a singer or other instrumentalist, they are also a valuable tool for understanding all the music you play.

Not all the strings will be strummed or played for each chord. An "x" above a string means to avoid playing that string.

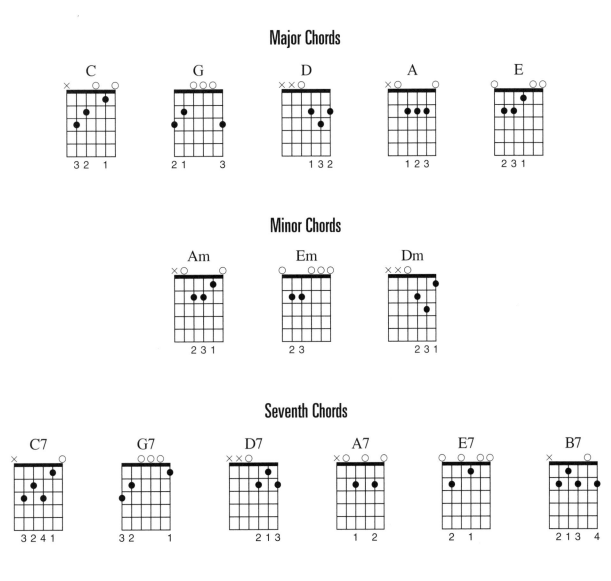

Strumming Chords

There are many ways to strum. It is the easiest and most common for guitarists to use their thumb or *p* to play a downward stroke from the low to the high strings. Use a combination of movement from both the thumb and the wrist to play each string with equal weight. This technique works well for certain settings, especially when an individual chord is played or when strumming a slow group of chords, as in the following example.

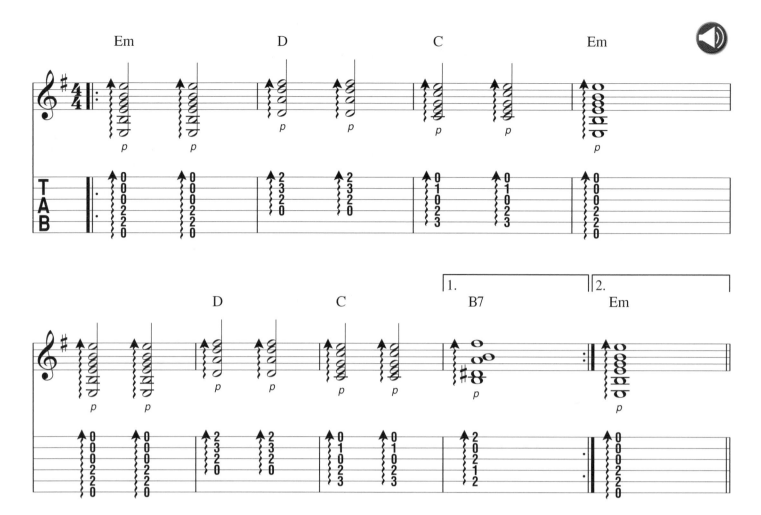

Don't be fooled by the direction of the arrow! The upward pointing arrow means a downstroke, because with the downstroke the strings are played from the lowest-sounding string to the highest-sounding string, as indicated by the arrow.

Two Common Chord Progressions

Strum four times per measure. One strum equals one quarter note in 4/4 time.

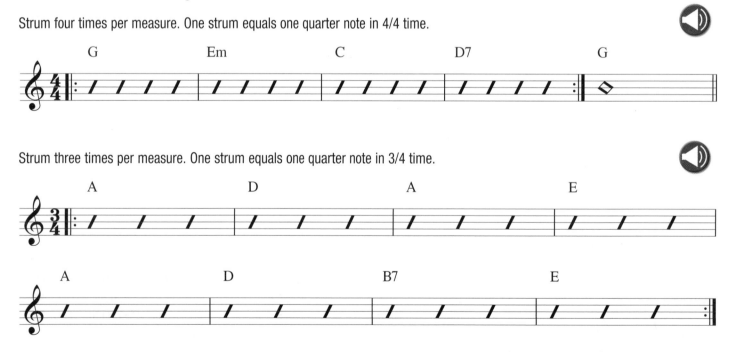

Strum three times per measure. One strum equals one quarter note in 3/4 time.

Rasgueado

For more active strumming, the beginning technique of the Spanish Flamenco strum, or *rasgueado*, is well suited. In the following example, the arrow indicates that the *i* finger alternates downward and upward strokes to play groups of eighth-note chords. Use movement from the big knuckle of your *i* finger and minimize the movement of your wrist and arm.

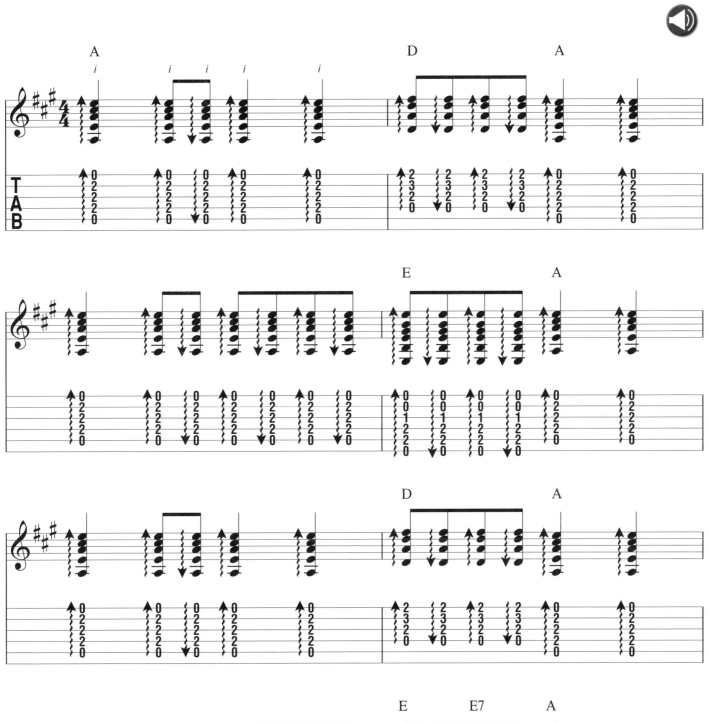

CHORDAL ACCOMPANIMENT

"Shenandoah" is a beautiful traditional American melody. A simple accompaniment could be realized by strumming the indicated chords four times per measure. For a more interesting accompaniment try the repeated right-hand arpeggio pattern *pima*, which repeats once per measure. Other patterns which fit in 4/4 time will also work well. Have fun experimenting!

SHENANDOAH

American Traditional

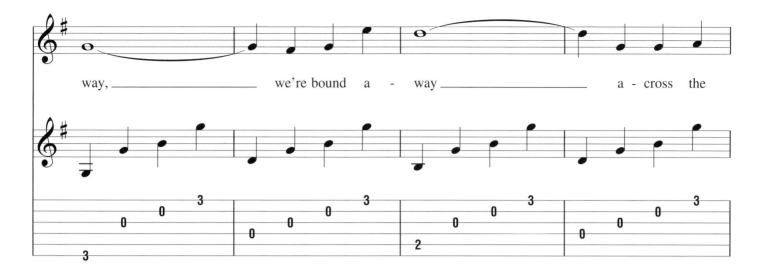

way, _____ we're bound a - way _____ a - cross the

wide _____ Mis - sour - i.

SIXTEENTH NOTES

As you have seen, the quarter note can be divided into two equal parts to create eighth notes. The quarter note can also be divided into four equal parts to create sixteenth notes. The sixteenth note is twice as fast as an eighth note and four times as fast as a quarter note. Both the sixteenth note and the sixteenth rest have two flags or beams.

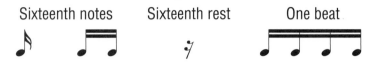

Rhythm Exercise — Sixteenth Notes

Play or clap the following exercise.

Here's a handy chart that shows the breakdown and division of note and rest values that we've covered.

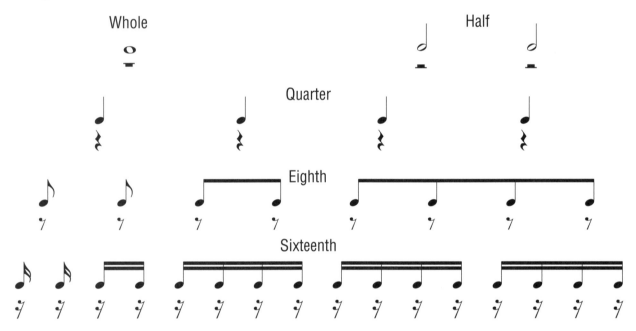

The following Allegro is in 4/4 time. This piece should be evenly played using the *pima* right-hand pattern. The bass notes should be accented slightly to bring out the moving voice. Practice slowly at first to keep a steady tempo.

Be sure to hold the quarter notes for their full duration while playing the following sixteenths.

ALLEGRO

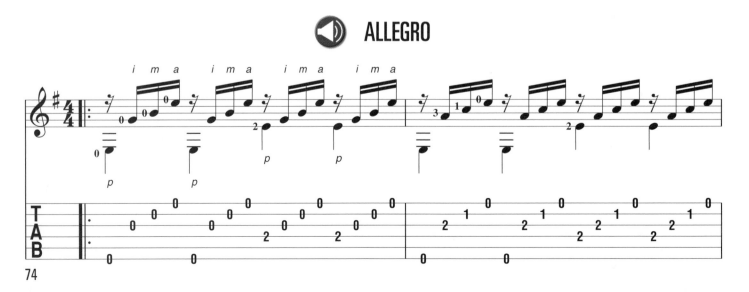

74

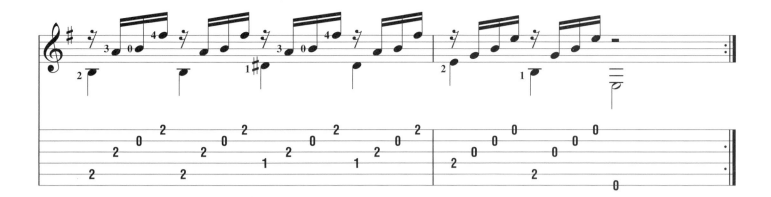

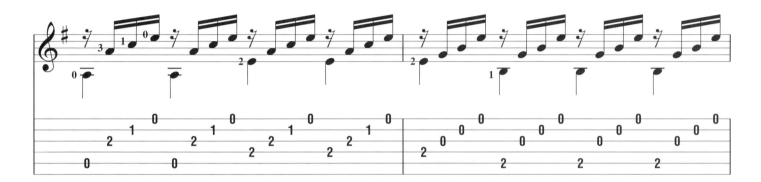

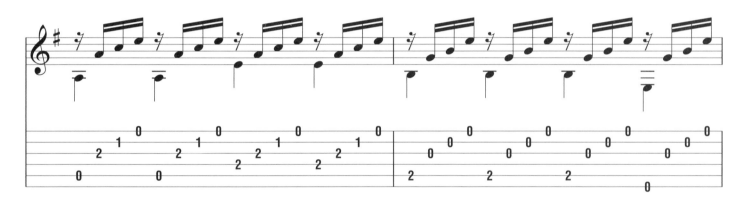

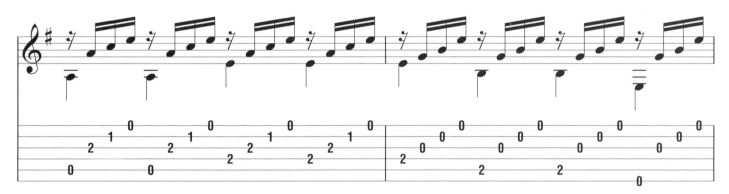

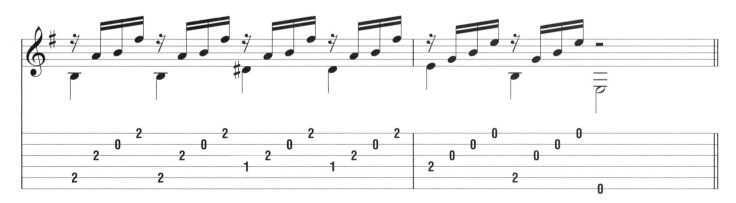

TRIPLETS

You have seen that quarter notes can be divided into two equal parts with eighth notes and four equal parts with sixteenth notes. Quarter notes can also be divided into three equal parts with triplets. Usually a numeral 3 will be written under or over the notes that are to be played as triplets. This indication may not always be continued if triplets appear repeatedly in a piece.

ANDANTINO

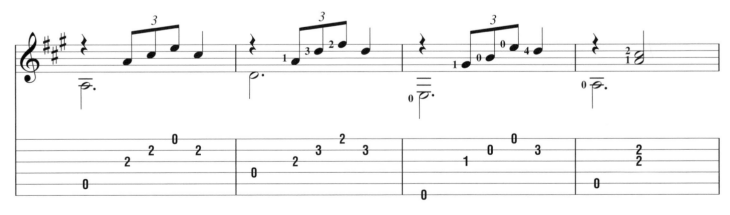

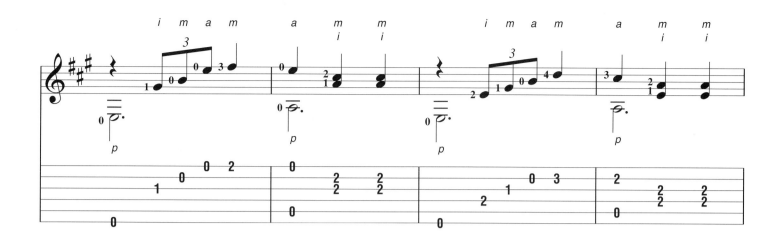

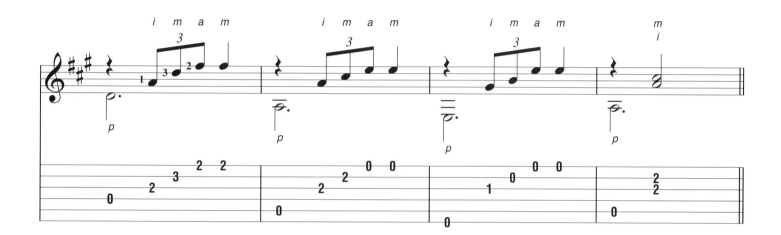

REST STROKE

Rest strokes give notes a rounder and louder tone.

As you have seen in some of the previous pieces, there are times that notes need to be accented. Rather than just playing these notes louder, the rest stroke can be used to give these notes a sound with more depth and power.

The rest stroke is sometimes called *apoyando*, a Spanish term. The free stroke is sometimes called *tirando*.

PLAYING THE REST STROKE

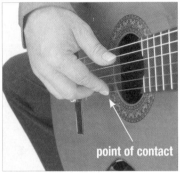

Rest Stroke Setup

Keeping your hand still, use the big knuckle of your index finger to push through the high E string, coming to rest on the adjacent B string. Relax your fingertip enough so that your finger can push through the completion of the stroke.

When the stroke is complete the finger should return to its original position just off the string. Practice this basic stroke with *i, m,* and *a* fingers. Keep your hand still and relaxed, letting the weight of your finger provide the power to generate the sound. Relax the finger after the stroke.

Rest Stroke Follow-Through

Alternating rest strokes with *i* and *m* is a common technique used by classical guitarists to highlight beautiful melodies. Often used in scale-like passages, it is important to strive for a consistent and full tone for each note. Be certain to continue to alternate even when changing strings.

Rest Stroke Exercises

Repeated rest strokes; alternate *i* and *m* on open strings. Practice these exercises with *m* and *a* as well. **The common symbol for the rest stroke is** V.

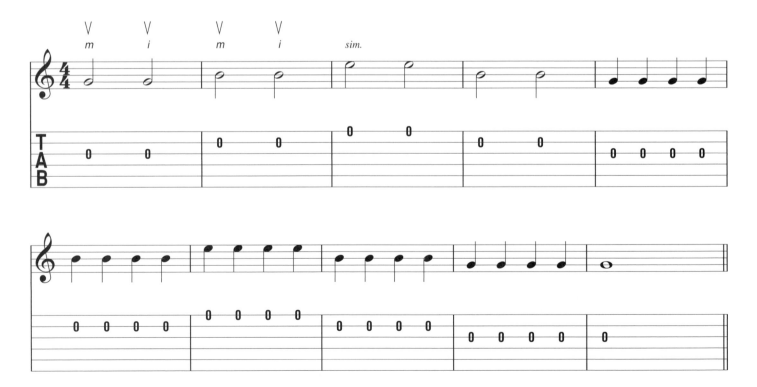

Repeated rest strokes with C scale; alternate *i* and *m*.

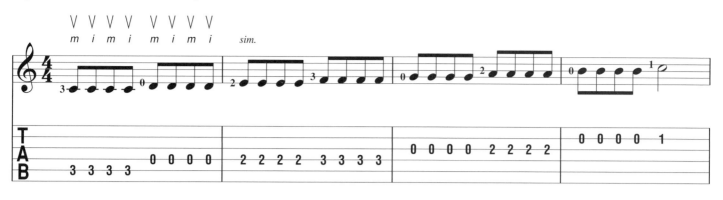

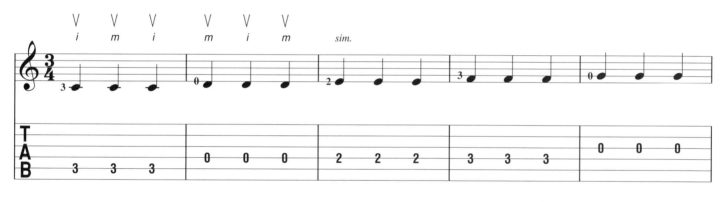

Here is a rhythmic variation on the C scale: groups of three. Again, play with *i* and *m* rest strokes.

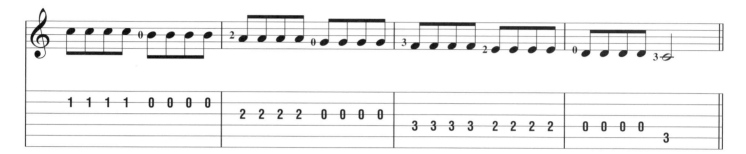

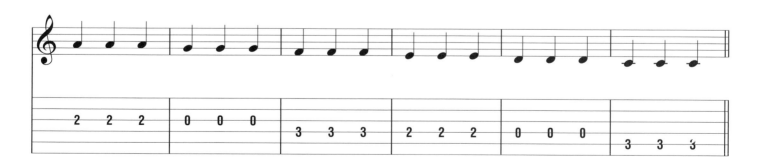

For this exercise use rest strokes with *a* and *m* and a free stroke for *p*.

Use an *a* finger rest stroke for this melody. Use an *im* free stroke for the accompaniment.

ESTUDIO

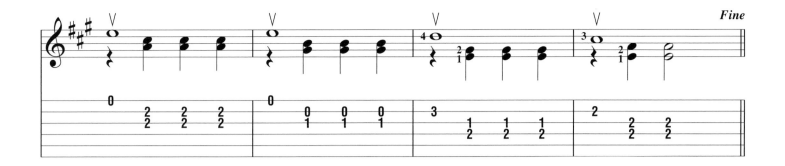

Fine

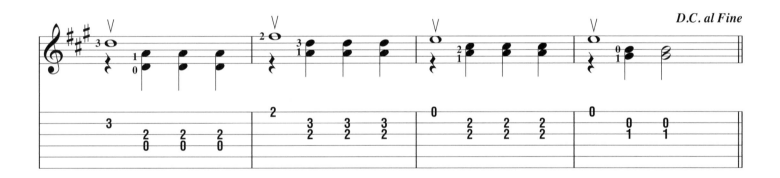

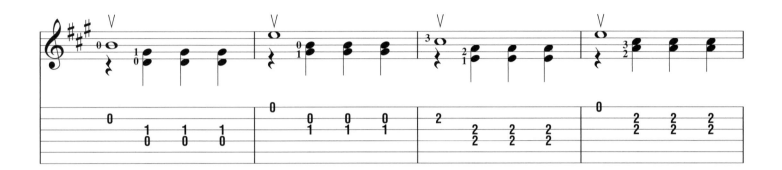

D.C. al Fine

To bring out the melody, use a rest stroke with the *a* finger on the upstemmed quarter notes.

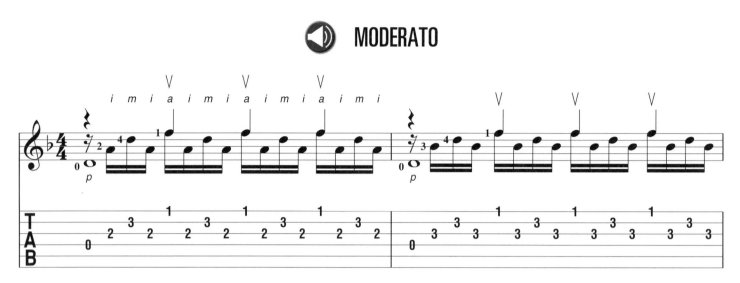

MODERATO

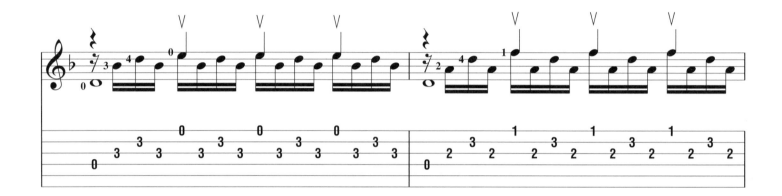

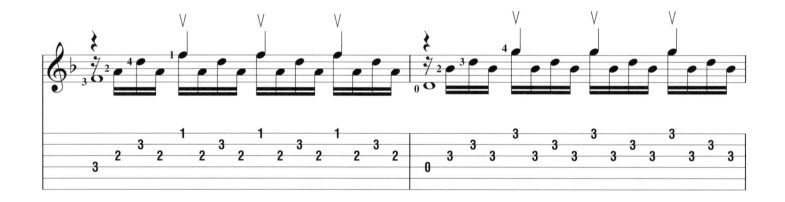

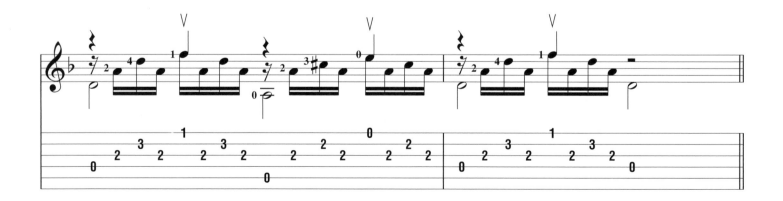

Finger Rest Stroke Together with Thumb Free Stroke

This important technique is a little challenging at first, but mastering it will add an extra dimension to your music, allowing you to emphasize important melody notes while keeping the accompaniment in the background. Before proceeding, it is imperative that you have mastered the rest stroke pieces and exercises in the previous section.

The following exercises use only open strings, allowing you to concentrate fully on the right-hand movements. Remember, the fingers follow through to complete the stroke on the adjacent string, while the thumb or *p* plays a normal free stroke.

Practice alternating *i* and *m*, then *m* and *a*.

Exercise 1

Exercise 2

Exercise 3

Exercise 4

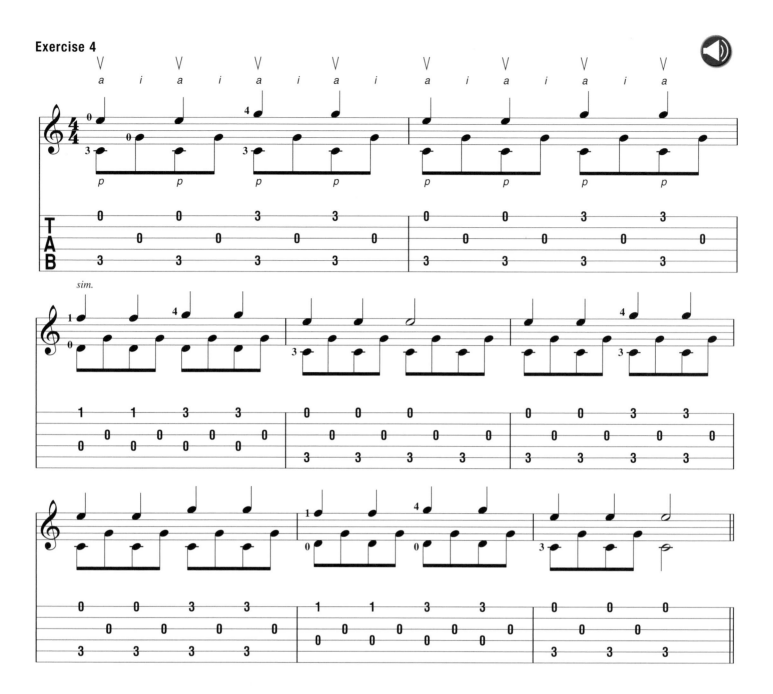

Following are some pieces that combine the rest stroke and free stroke.

CANCIÓN

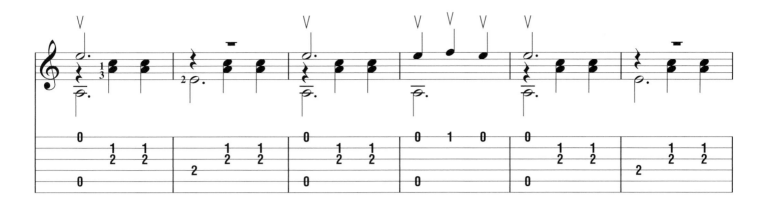

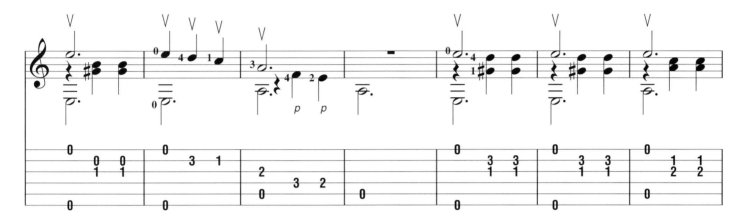

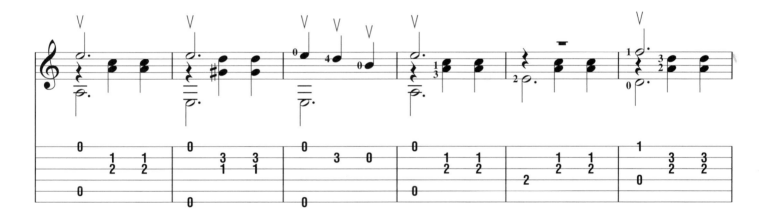

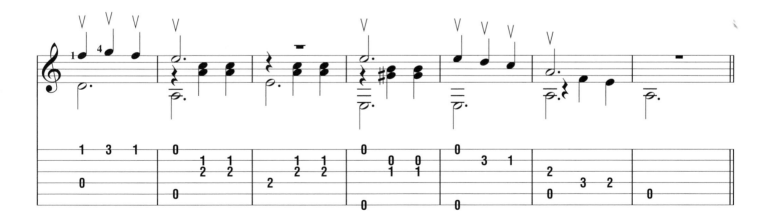

SERENATA

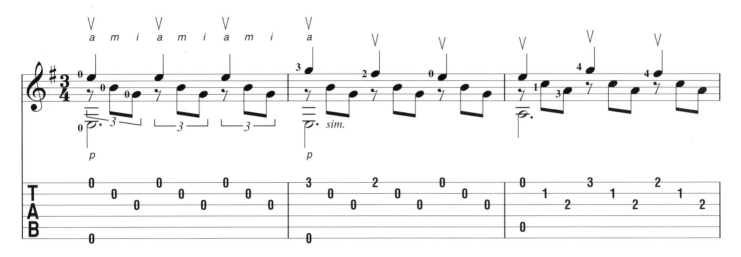

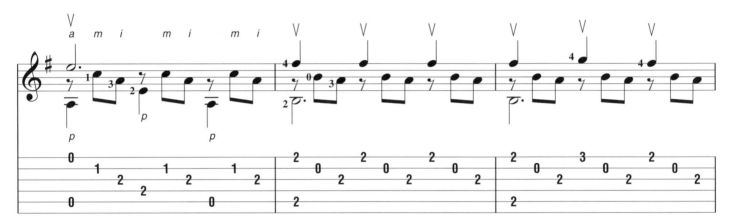

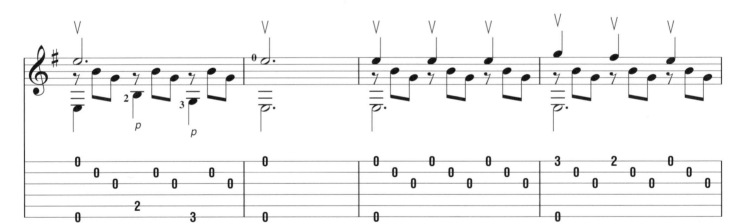

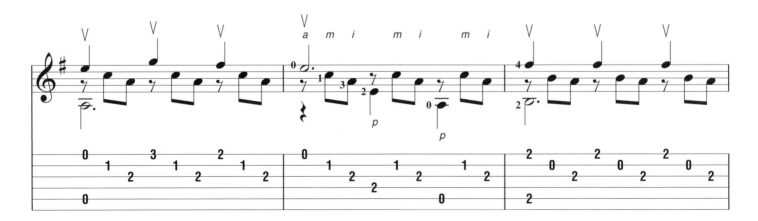

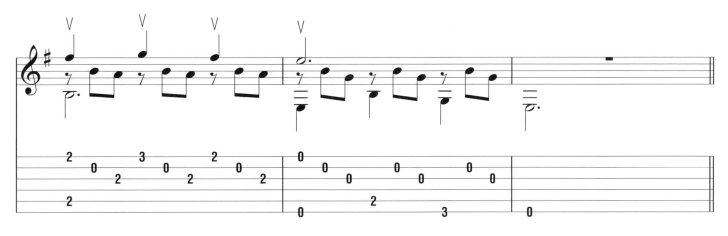

THUMB REST STROKE

There are times when the thumb needs to play the melody or other important accented notes. For this the thumb rest stroke can be used. This stroke is not as commonly used as the finger rest stroke, but it is equally important when needed and is an essential part of a guitarist's technique.

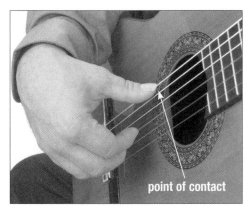

Thumb Rest Stroke Setup

Thumb Rest Stroke Follow-Through

Using the thumb rest stroke, practice the next theme with attention to the rhythm. Focus on achieving a legato melody. On the audio track, the following three examples are played in succession with no pause.

After mastering the above melody, add the accompaniment while keeping the thumb rest strokes.

VARIATION I

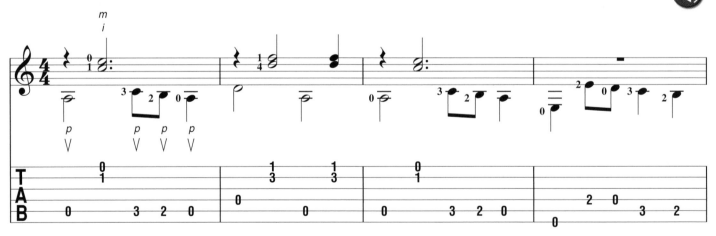

Variation II has a slightly different rhythm and melody. Practice just the melody first before adding the accompaniment.

VARIATION II

MOORISH CARAVAN

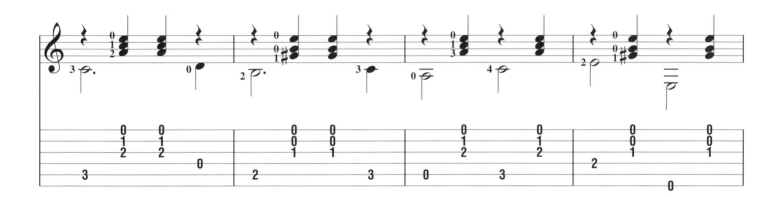

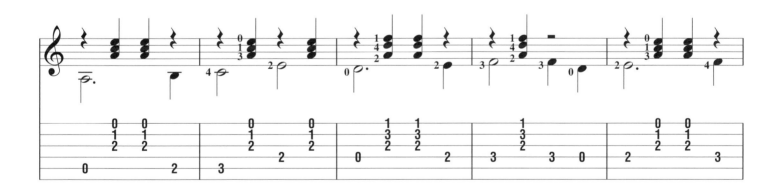

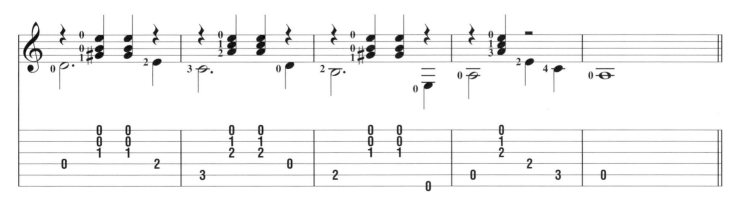

PASSACAGLIA

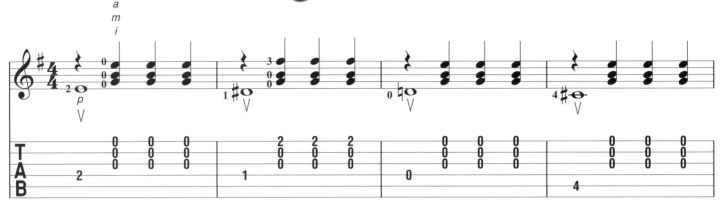

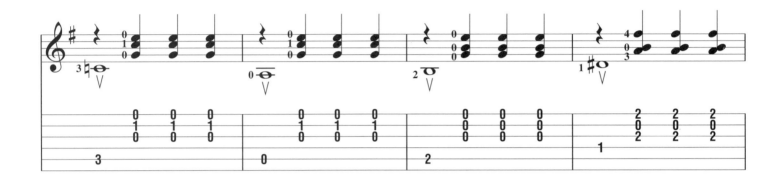

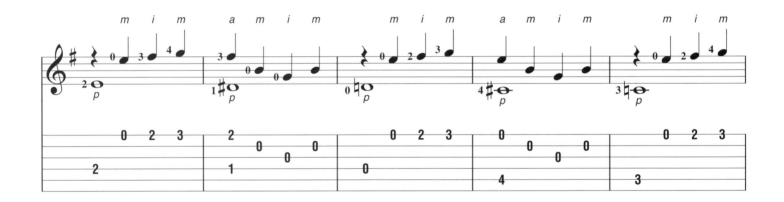

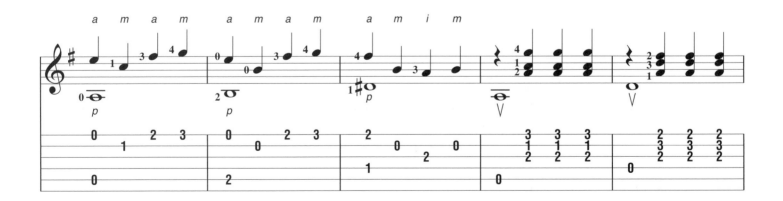

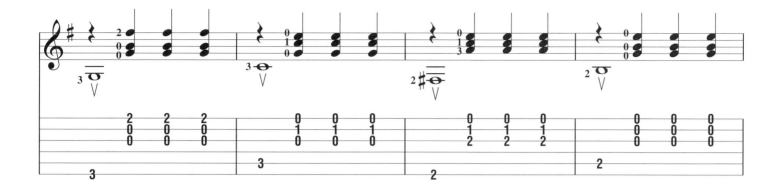

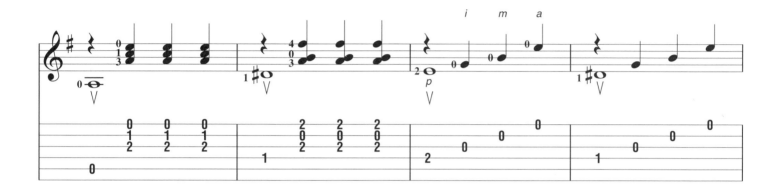

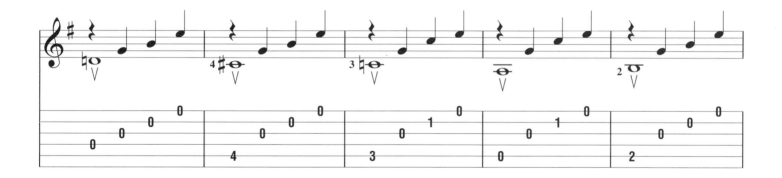

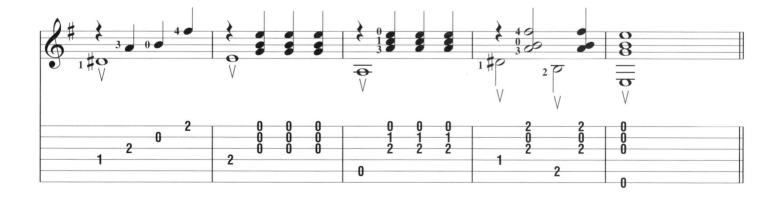

SLURS

The *slur* is an articulation technique that guitarists use to sound notes with the left hand. It helps to create a smooth, connected, legato sound between two notes, similar to a violinist playing several notes in succession with only one bow stroke. Ascending slurs are also known as *hammer-ons*; descending slurs are also known as *pull-offs.* Both types of slur are indicated in the music by a curved line connecting the two notes.

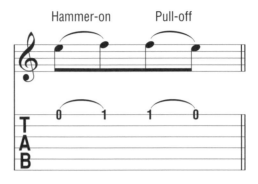

ASCENDING SLURS

To play an ascending slur (hammer-on), play the first note in the normal way on either an open or fretted string. While this note is still ringing, hammer your left-hand fingertip down perpendicularly onto the desired higher pitch with enough velocity to sound the second note. Use only as much force as is needed to sound the second note, which will not be quite as loud as the first. This is part of the musical idea of the guitar slur.

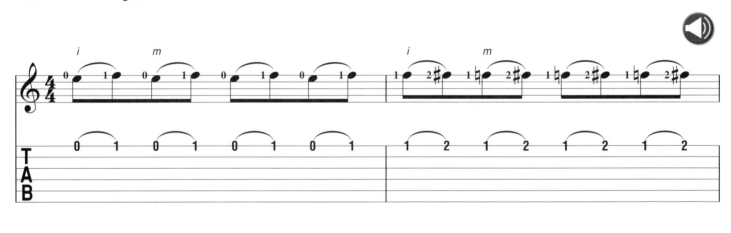

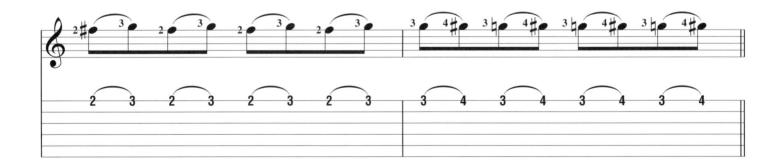

Prelude No. 7

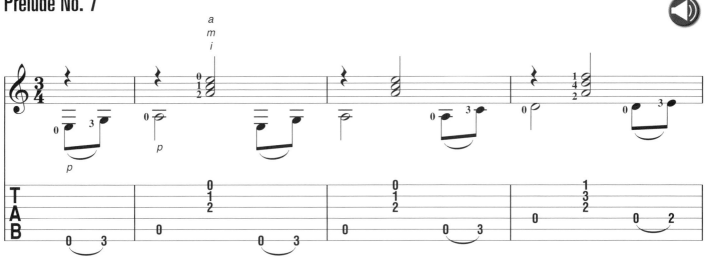

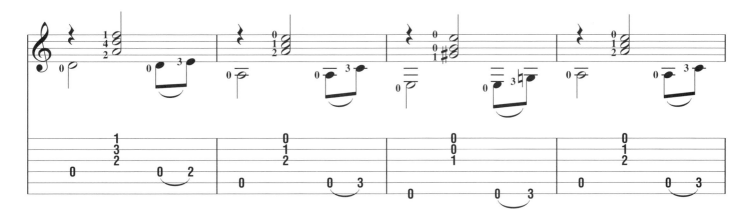

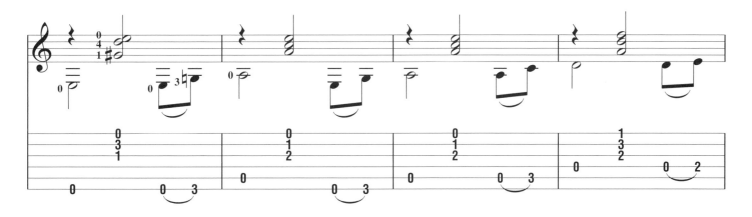

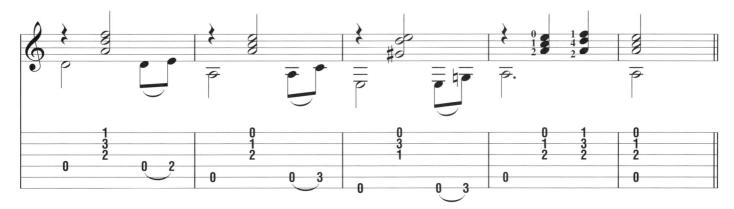

DESCENDING SLURS

To play a descending slur (pull-off), your left-hand finger should pull off the string with a little downward motion (toward the floor), so you're basically plucking the string with your left hand. If you simply release your finger from the string, you won't produce enough sound. If you play a few repeated descending slurs you will notice that your fingertip will travel in a circular path as it returns to the string to play. **If you are playing descending slurs ending on a fretted rather than an open string, place both fingers down on their respective notes before beginning the slur.**

Before you try the following exercises it is a good idea to review the position of the left hand and fingers. Fingers must be poised over the strings, and all the fingers need to remain naturally curved rather than straightening or reaching to play the notes. Descending slurs are a bit more challenging than ascending slurs. Practice the exercises slowly at first with care for correct finger placement and attention to maintaining an even rhythm.

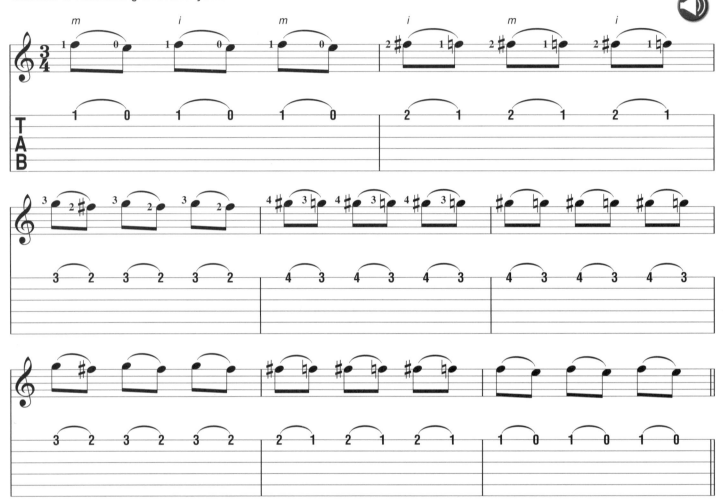

Use rest strokes for all upstemmed melody notes in the next example.

GAVOTTE

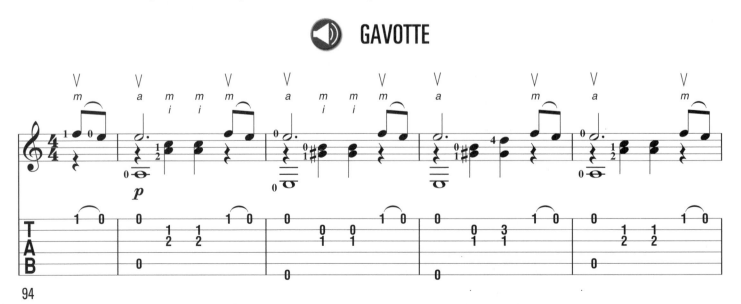

The following exercise contains both ascending and descending slurs. This and the previous slur exercises should be practiced on each string. Besides learning a new technique that will enhance your playing, these exercises will help to build strength and agility in your left hand.

Slur Exercise

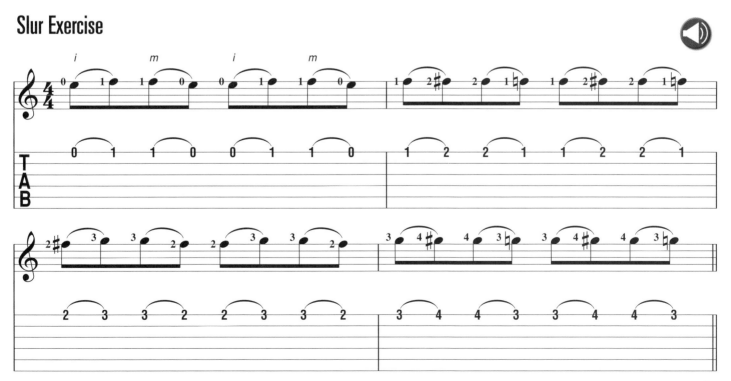

MORE PIECES

CIRCLED NUMBERS AND EQUIVALENT NOTES

In measure 3 of the following piece you will find a new notation, a circled number. The circled number 3 indicates that the B note should be played on the 4th fret of the third string rather than on the open B, thus allowing the following D note to be played on a different string, and enabling the B note to ring for its full duration. This fingering also lets the right hand continue with its *pimi* pattern.

The Estudio by Aguado features a slow but haunting melody in the bass. Use an accented thumb stroke to bring out this voice.

Dionysio Aguado (1784–1849)

A Spanish guitar virtuoso, Aguado wrote a variety of important works for guitar including dazzling concert works, a collection of studies, and a highly regarded method book, *Méthode Complète pour la Guitare*. He lived in Paris for several years where he collaborated with another famous Spanish guitarist, Fernando Sor. He spent the last ten years of his life in his homeland Spain.

ESTUDIO IN A MINOR

Dionysio Aguado

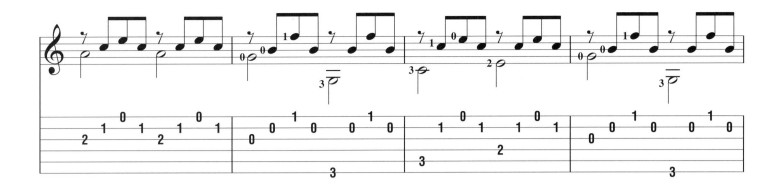

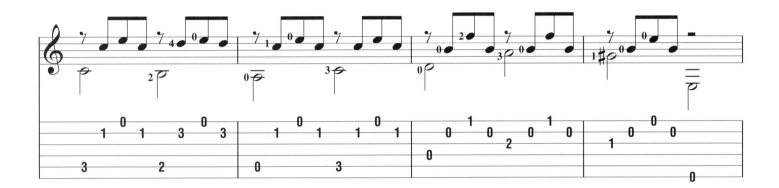

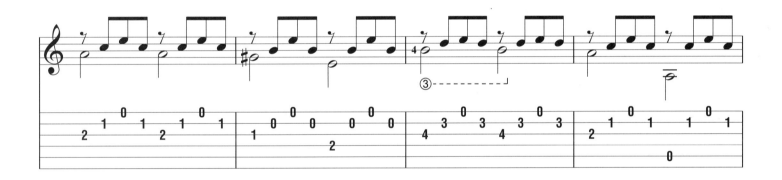

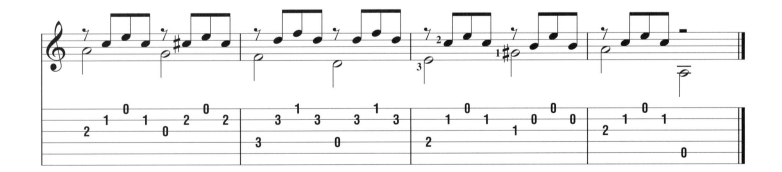

CHANSON

French Folksong

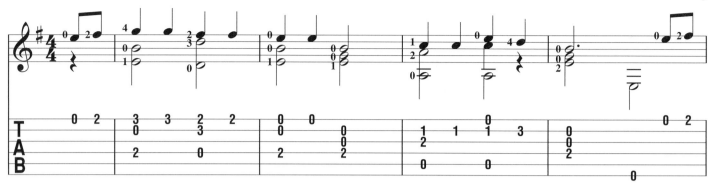

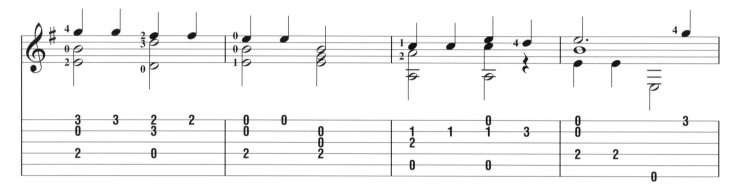

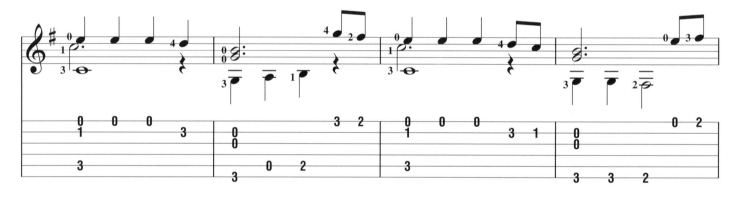

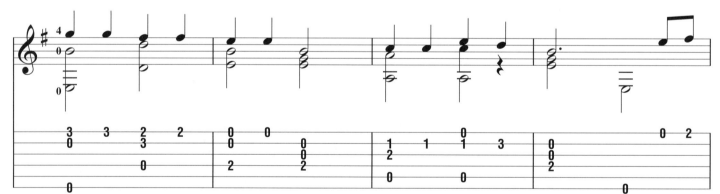

rit.

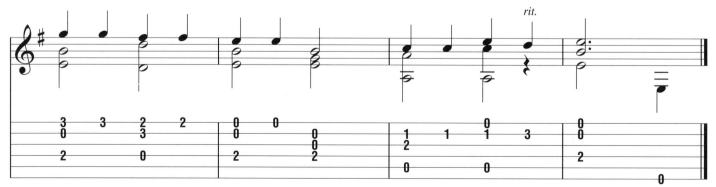

Malagueña is a traditional Spanish dance with roots in Málaga, a city in the Andalucia province on the Costa del Sol coast of Spain. Malagueña originated as an improvised folk dance among the Sevillian gypsies in Andalucia. Like much of the music in the Flamenco style, it uses the rhythms and melodies that date back centuries to the Moorish invasion.

MALAGUEÑA

Spanish Traditional

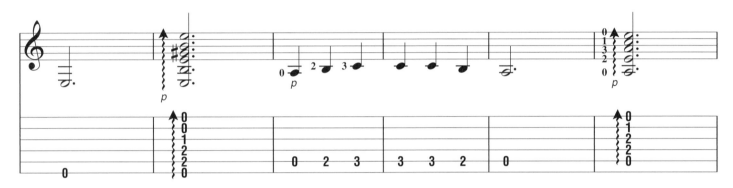

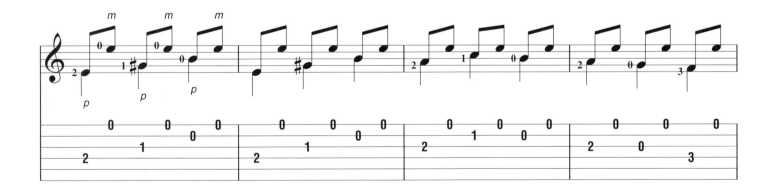

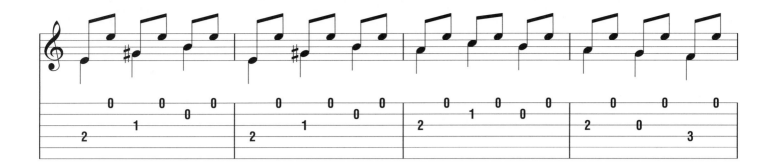

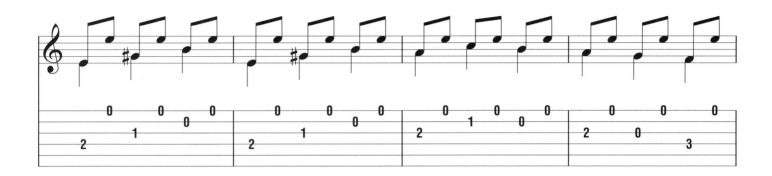

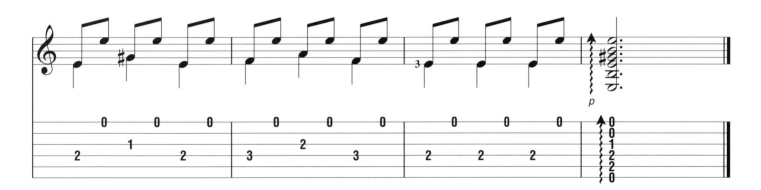

You are now familiar with all the notes in first position, but by learning one more note (the high A) you will be able to increase the number of pieces you can play and get a feel for playing the notes in higher positions. Playing the A note requires shifting. This means shifting your entire left hand, including your thumb, allowing the 4th finger to naturally fall on the 5th fret of the high E string. Don't forget to shift back when returning to your original position.

Henry Purcell (1659–1695)

Henry Purcell is one of England's most prestigious composers. He spent much of his short life as a composer, organist, and singer in the service of three different kings over a 25-year period at the Chapel Royal at Westminster Abbey. While he never wrote any music for guitar, he did compose for nearly every type of important setting in England's Baroque time period. He died in 1695, a year after composing funeral music for Queen Mary.

▶ MINUET

Henry Purcell

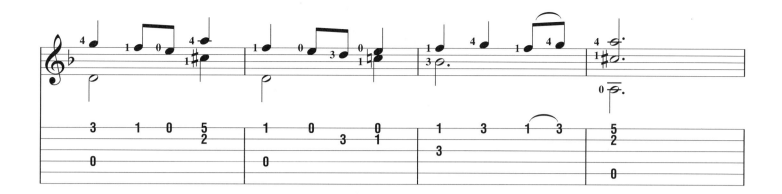

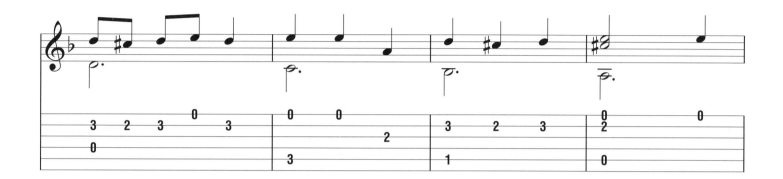

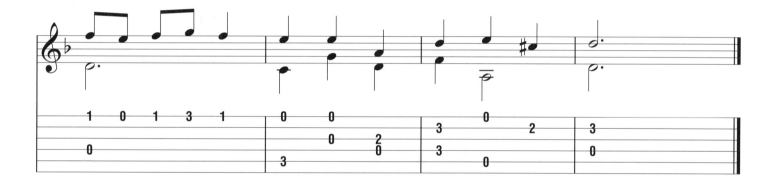

FERMATA

When this musical symbol called the *fermata* is placed above or below a note or chord, it is an instruction to the player to hold those notes a little longer than the written duration.

VALS

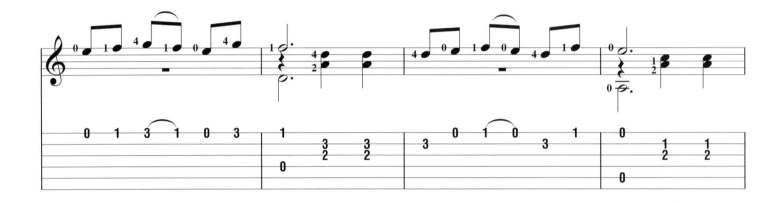

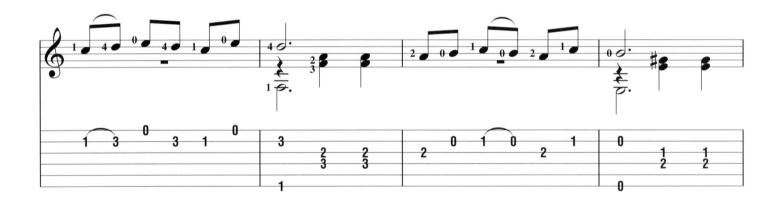

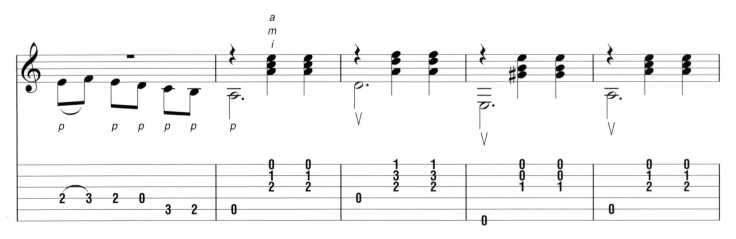

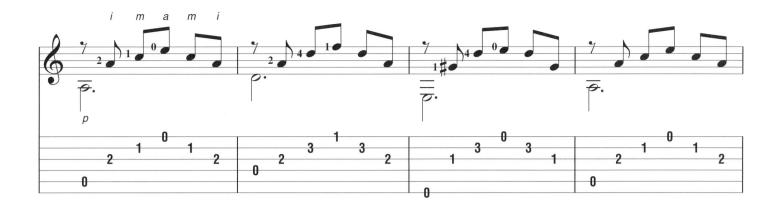

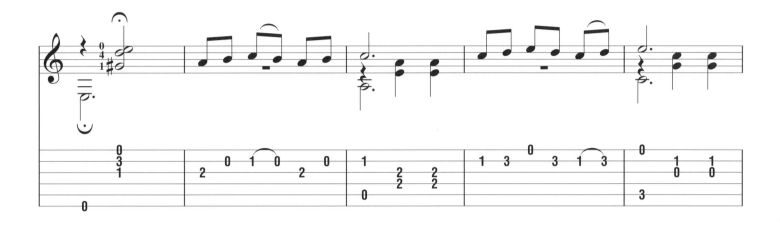

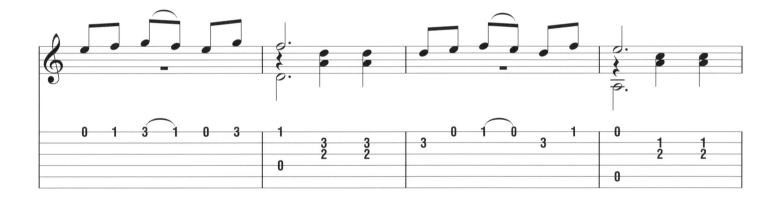

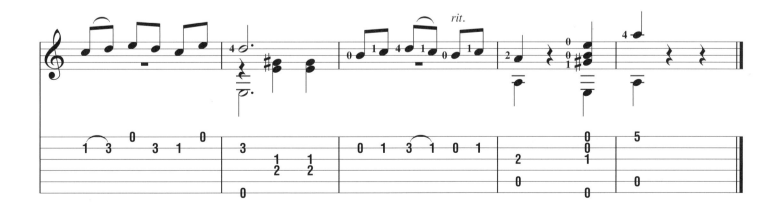

ANDANTE

Ferdinando Carulli

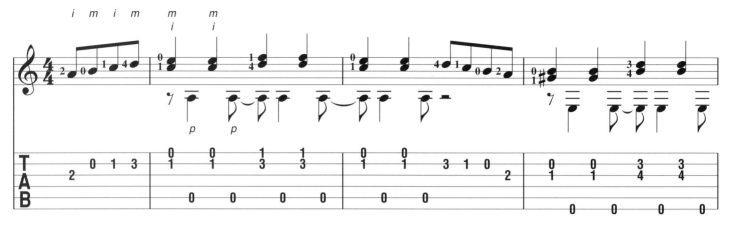

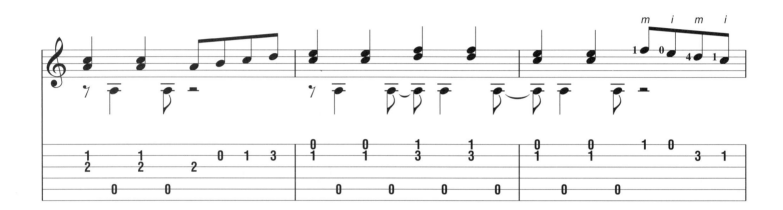

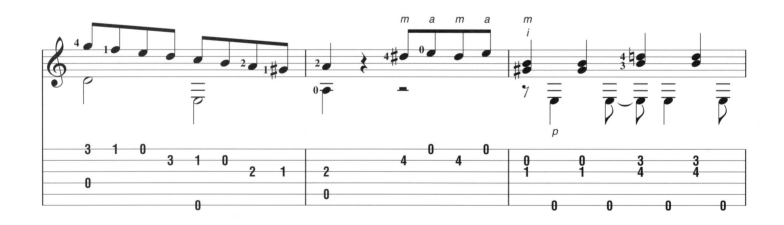

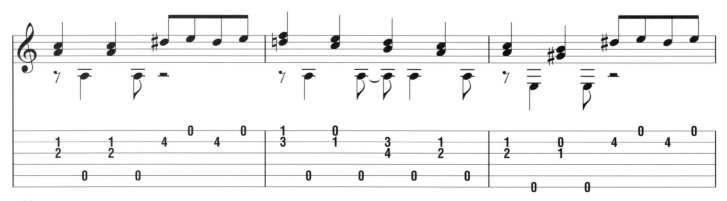

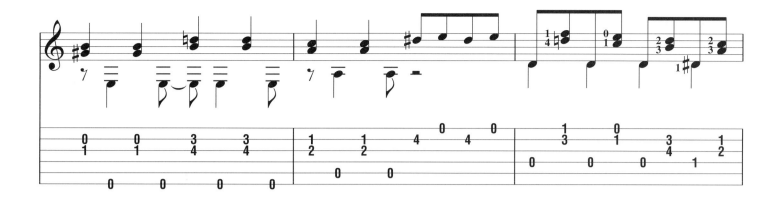

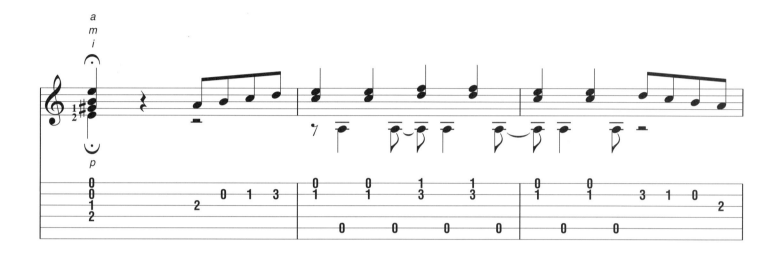

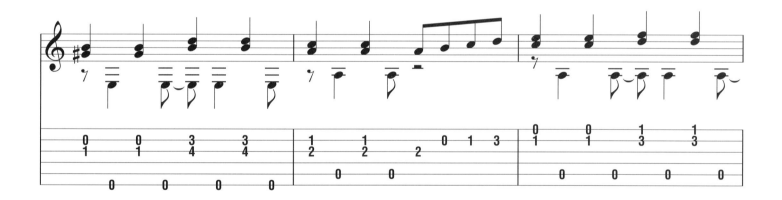

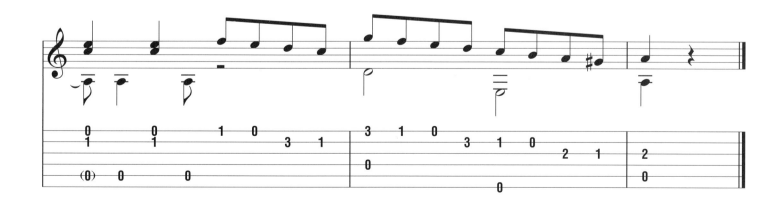

Ludwig van Beethoven (1770–1827)

Along with Mozart and Bach, Ludwig van Beethoven has reached the highest level of musical achievement in the minds of music lovers. The son of a court musician, Beethoven was born in Bonn, Germany in 1770. At the age of twelve he had his first music published. By 1792, at the age of 22, he set off to the musical capital of Vienna which was to be his home for the rest of his life. An innovator bridging the Classical and Romantic eras, he is remembered for his many emotionally powerful and dynamic masterpieces. He continued to compose and conduct even after he began to go deaf at age 28.

"I have never thought of writing for reputation and honor. What I have in my heart must come out; that is the reason why I compose."
–Ludwig van Beethoven

ODE TO JOY

Ludwig van Beethoven

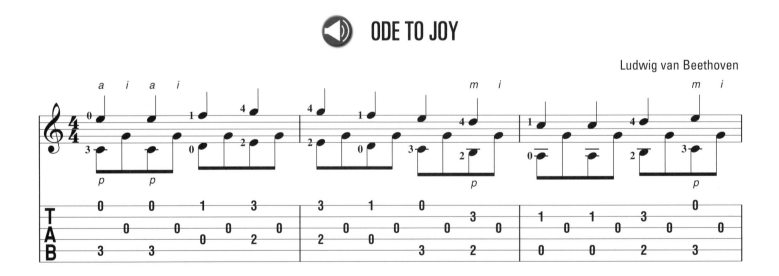

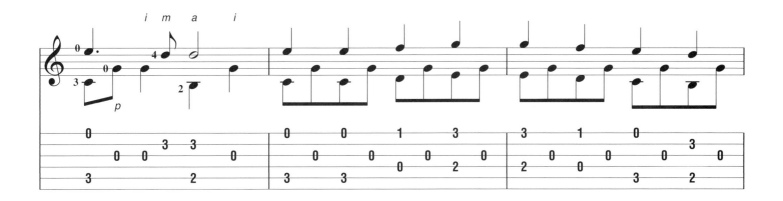

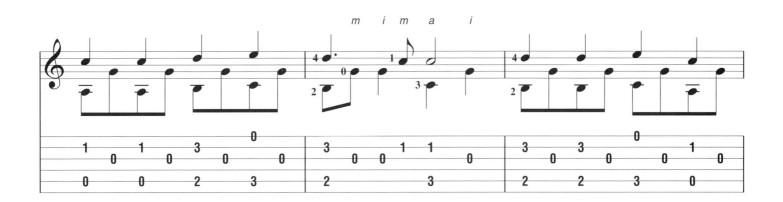

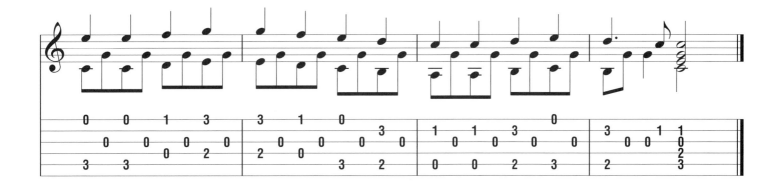

AIR

Paul Henry

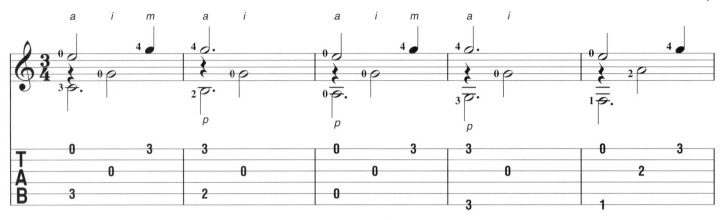

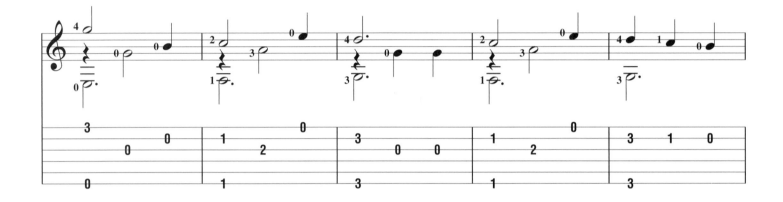

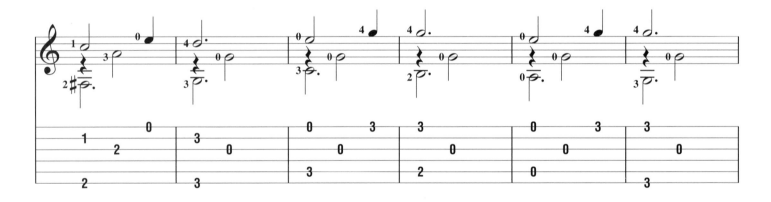

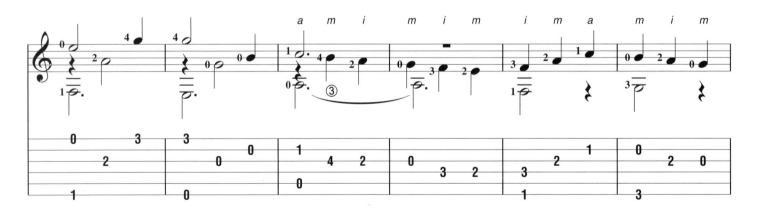

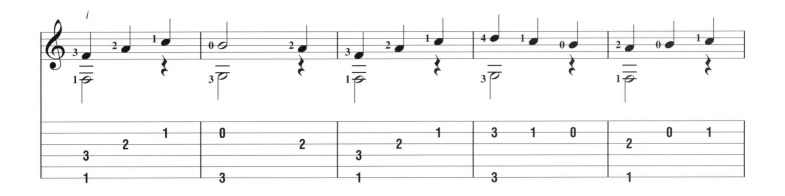

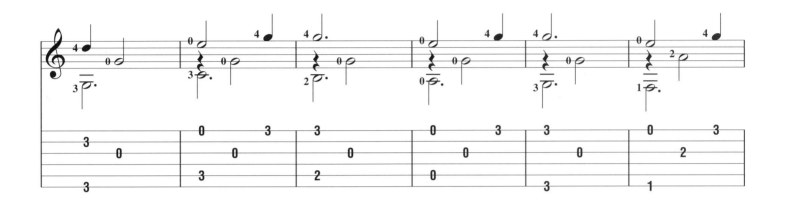

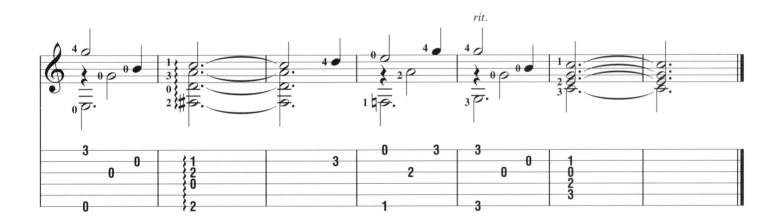

"Greensleeves" is perhaps the most famous of all early English folk songs from the Renaissance period. Legend tells us that it may have been written by King Henry VIII (1491–1547). Notice the new note F# on the fourth string, fourth fret. Play this note with your fourth finger. "Greensleeves" is in 6/8. Try to feel the beat on the dotted quarter note.

GREENSLEEVES

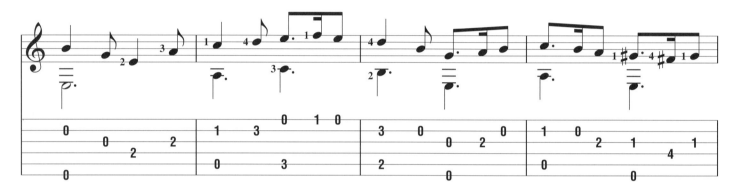

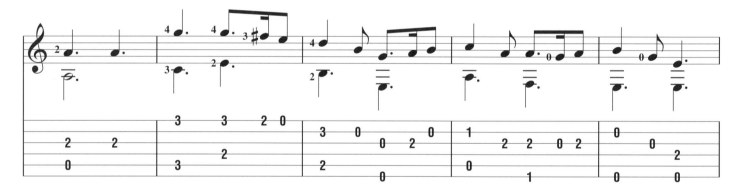

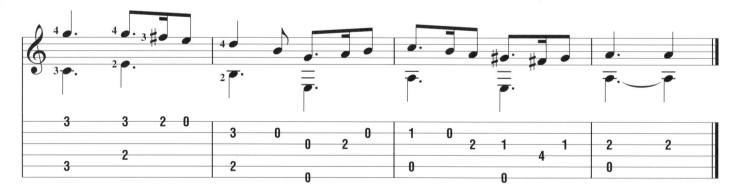

Johann Sebastian Bach (1685–1750)

Born into a distinguished musical family with generations of noted composers and musicians, Johann Sebastian Bach achieved the most prominence and is considered one of the greatest composers in history. He was taught by his father how to play the violin and harpsichord. He held several prestigious local positions as court musician and composer in Arnstadt, Weimar, Köthen, and as cantor and director of music at Leipzig. A virtuoso organist, he gained fame throughout Germany during his career, but since the 19th century he has been hailed as a genius whose work represents the peak of the Baroque era.

MINUET

Johann Sebastian Bach

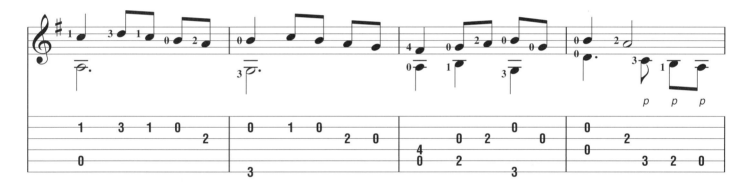

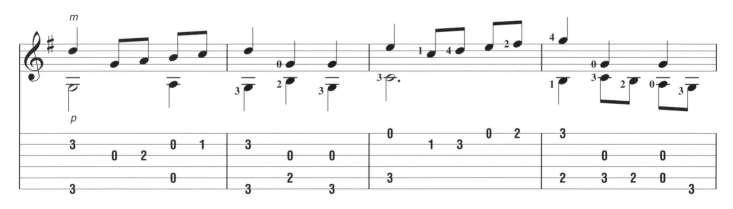

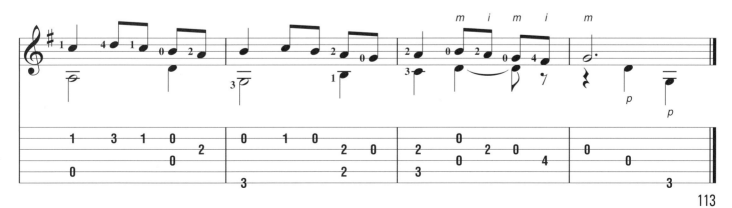

Wolfgang Amadeus Mozart (1756–1793)

The musical genius Mozart began composing by the age of five in his hometown of Salzburg, Austria. Encouraged by his father Leopold, the six-year-old Mozart and his elder sister performed many concerts in European courts. By the time he was nine, he published his first piece and began writing symphonies. Realizing that to achieve success he would have to leave Salzburg, Mozart left in 1777 for Munich, Mannheim, and later Paris looking for a position equal to his talents. Never professionally satisfied but still managing to survive on his talents, he went on to compose a wealth of over 600 beautiful and unique works which include operas, symphonies, concertos, and masses. In the music world, it is perhaps Mozart's star that shines the brightest.

THEME IN A

Wolfgang Amadeus Mozart

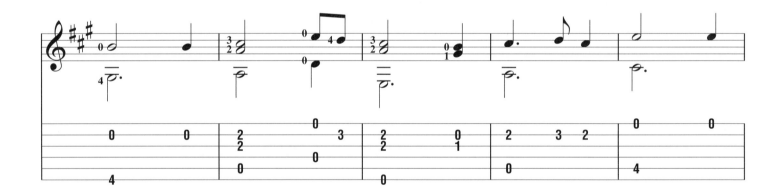

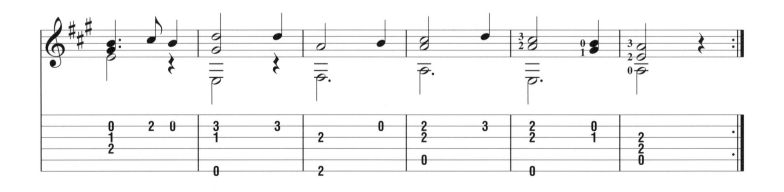

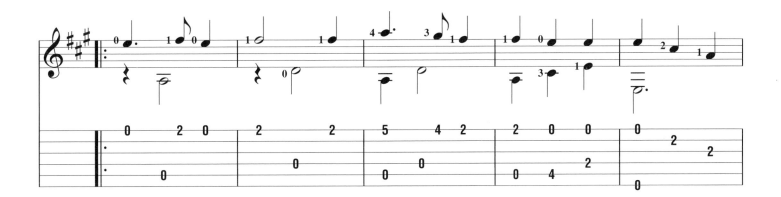

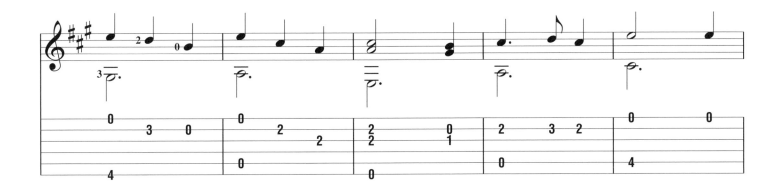

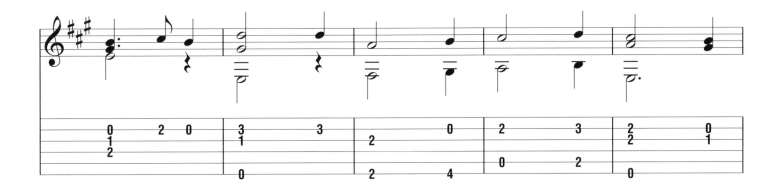

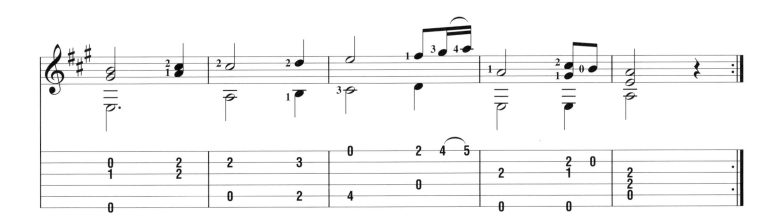

REFERENCE SECTION

USE OF THE FINGERNAILS

While nearly all advanced players use the fingernails of the right hand to produce the sound, it is recommended for the first few months of learning the guitar that you use the flesh of your fingertip and keep your nails short. This will allow you to get a good feel of the string sliding off the fingertip in a controlled manner without getting snagged or caught on the nail. When you feel secure with the skill that your right hand has developed, you may consider using the nails. Correct use of the nails will create more brilliance, volume, speed, and clarity in your playing.

Every guitarist has differently-shaped hands and nails, so describing the best way for any individual player to shape his or her nails is not realistic; however, below are some of the basic concepts for grooming and use of the nails.

Grooming

Basic Nail Shape

The nails should basically follow the contour of your finger and thumb tips, extending about one-sixteenth of an inch beyond your fingertips.

Use a fine grade emery board or 500 grit sanding paper to smooth out any irregularities. All the edges, top, and underneath must be smooth.

Finger Contact Point

Placement on the String

In the correctly-placed contact point the nail and the flesh of your fingertip touch the string together on the left side of your fingertip. As your finger pushes through the string, the nail will slide though the string toward the center and release.

Thumb Contact Point and Release Point

Thumb Contact Point

The thumb will start its placement closer to the center of the nail or tip and slide off the nail further to the left side.

Take care with both the fingers and thumb to avoid catching or hooking the nail. Keep an ear out for any unpleasant, tinny sounds or raspiness. If this occurs try to reshape or smooth out the offending area of the nail. Finding the exact shape and routine of caring for your right-hand nails will take some experimentation and patience.

TAKING CARE OF YOUR GUITAR

You should expect that your guitar will last to give you years of musical service, but of course certain precautions need to be taken with any valued instrument. The number one cause of major damage to a solid wood instrument is too little humidity. Be sure to keep your guitar in an environment that stays above a humidity level of 35%. If the humidity falls below this level for a few days the wood will begin to shrink, and your guitar will be in danger of cracking. If you live in an arid environment use a guitar humidifier (they can be purchased inexpensively at most music stores) or take steps to control your humidity at the room or house level. Too much humidity is not good for your guitar either. This will swell the wood and could also have an adverse effect on the glues in your guitar. Less-expensive guitars that are constructed with mostly laminated woods are far less affected be these humidity changes.

Select a sturdy case for your guitar. The hardshell cases offer much greater protection for your instrument than the softcover cases or gig bags. You will also find that there will be substantially less wear and tear on your guitar when taking it in and out of its case with the hardshell case. Most importantly, keep it inside the case when not in use.

Most guitars have a fairly durable finish which will polish up nicely with just a slightly damp soft cloth; a light commercial polish will help as well.

To insure that your strings last for their maximum lifespan, it is recommended that you always play with clean hands and wipe your strings after playing with a damp, lint-free cloth. This will keep your bass strings free of dirt, debris, and perspiration.

CHANGING STRINGS ON YOUR CLASSICAL GUITAR

When to change strings is really a matter of personal opinion, however after about a month of practicing steadily for an hour or so a day, a fresh set of strings will really perk up the sound of your guitar. Changing your strings for the first time can be an adventure, but an important and unavoidable skill to master.

Be certain to buy the correct strings for your instrument! Classical guitars must have nylon or classical strings and acoustic steel-string guitars need steel strings. If in doubt, **ask an expert**. Most music stores offer many different types of strings and brands, and the options may confuse even a store clerk.

You will want to remove and then replace one string at a time. This procedure will keep the tension on the neck, bridge, and soundboard more constant and be a less traumatic experience for your guitar. You can also use the attached strings as reference for the changing procedure.

Turn the tuning peg clockwise to completely loosen the string, then detach it on both ends. Thread the new string through the bridge hole leaving enough length (about 1 1/2 inches) to wrap the string around itself as shown in the accompanying photos. Bass strings will have one loop as shown. Treble strings should be looped twice to avoid slippage. Be sure the last loop is lying snugly on the backside of the bridge rather than on top.

Bridge First Loop

Bridge Second Loop (for treble strings)

Bridge Final

Pull the string a bit to put some tension on the loop and thread the other end of the string through the appropriate roller of the machine heads. Loop the string around itself two times.

Keep a little tension on the string as you wind it (counter-clockwise) tight enough to be secure.

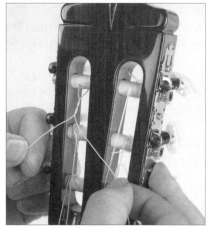

Headstock Loop

GUIDE TO STRINGS AND NOTES

Strings are referred to by letter name or by number: E–A–D–G–B–E, or 6–5–4–3–2–1. Notes use the alphabet from A to G. Notice in the diagram that from E to F and from B to C is only a one-fret distance. These are the natural half steps. The other notes are divided by natural whole steps.

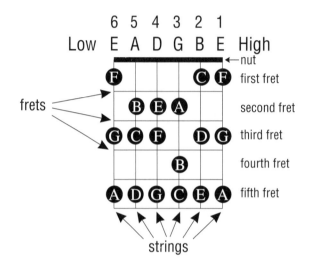

Here we see all the open-string notes as they appear on the staff.

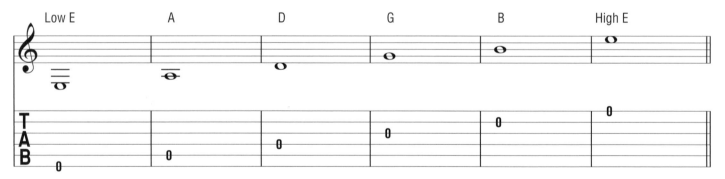

Finally, here are all the natural notes available on the guitar in open position, with the addition of the high A on the fifth fret of string 1.

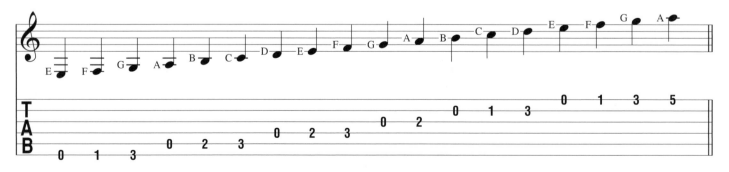

ACKNOWLEDGMENTS

I wish to sincerely give due credit to all of the students that I have taught over the decades. Helping them develop and improve has provided me with a wealth of concepts and ideas. Also I must thank colleagues Petar Kodzas, Kevin Hart, Rozanne Wilson-Marsh, and Julie Goldberg for their valuable contributions in the final stages of this method.

ABOUT THE AUTHOR

Paul Henry has been teaching guitar since the age of 15. Many of his students have developed their own successful musical careers in both performance and pedagogy. His students, ranging from age five to adulthood, have won first prizes in many local, national, and international competitions. He has conducted master classes at many colleges and universities throughout the United States and is on the faculty of Roosevelt University's Chicago Conservatory of Performing Arts, Concordia University in River Forest, Illinois, and the Metropolis' School of Performing Arts in Arlington Heights, Illinois. He has concertized throughout the U.S. and has several recordings to his credit. A graduate of the Cincinnati College-Conservatory and Ithaca College, he also was a student of Andrés Segovia in a series of master classes held at the University of Southern California. Segovia praised Henry for his "finesse and great sense of musicality with his instrument."

HAL LEONARD GUITAR METHOD

THE HAL LEONARD GUITAR METHOD is designed for anyone just learning to play acoustic or electric guitar. It is based on years of teaching guitar students of all ages, and it also reflects some of the best guitar teaching ideas from around the world. This comprehensive method includes: A learning sequence carefully paced with clear instructions; popular songs which increase the incentive to learn to play; versatility – can be used as self-instruction or with a teacher; audio accompaniments so that students have fun and sound great while practicing.

BOOK 1
00699010	Book Only	$8.99
00699027	Book/Online Audio	$12.99
00697341	Book/Online Audio + DVD	$24.99
00697318	DVD Only	$19.99
00155480	Deluxe Beginner Edition (Book, CD, DVD, Online Audio/ Video & Chord Poster)	$19.99

COMPLETE (BOOKS 1, 2 & 3)
00699040	Book Only	$16.99
00697342	Book/Online Audio	$24.99

BOOK 2
00699020	Book Only	$8.99
00697313	Book/Online Audio	$12.99

BOOK 3
00699030	Book Only	$8.99
00697316	Book/Online Audio	$12.99

Prices, contents and availability subject to change without notice.

STYLISTIC METHODS

ACOUSTIC GUITAR
00697347	Method Book/Online Audio	$17.99
00237969	Songbook/Online Audio	$16.99

BLUEGRASS GUITAR
00697405	Method Book/Online Audio	$16.99

BLUES GUITAR
00697326	Method Book/Online Audio (9" x 12")	$16.99
00697344	Method Book/Online Audio (6" x 9")	$15.99
00697385	Songbook/Online Audio (9" x 12")	$14.99
00248636	Kids Method Book/Online Audio	$12.99

BRAZILIAN GUITAR
00697415	Method Book/Online Audio	$17.99

CHRISTIAN GUITAR
00695947	Method Book/Online Audio	$16.99
00697408	Songbook/CD Pack	$14.99

CLASSICAL GUITAR
00697376	Method Book/Online Audio	$15.99

COUNTRY GUITAR
00697337	Method Book/Online Audio	$22.99
00697400	Songbook/Online Audio	$19.99

FINGERSTYLE GUITAR
00697378	Method Book/Online Audio	$21.99
00697432	Songbook/Online Audio	$16.99

FLAMENCO GUITAR
00697363	Method Book/Online Audio	$15.99

FOLK GUITAR
00697414	Method Book/Online Audio	$16.99

JAZZ GUITAR
00695359	Book/Online Audio	$22.99
00697386	Songbook/Online Audio	$15.99

JAZZ-ROCK FUSION
00697387	Book/Online Audio	$24.99

R&B GUITAR
00697356	Book/Online Audio	$19.99
00697433	Songbook/CD Pack	$14.99

ROCK GUITAR
00697319	Book/Online Audio	$16.99
00697383	Songbook/Online Audio	$16.99

ROCKABILLY GUITAR
00697407	Book/Online Audio	$16.99

OTHER METHOD BOOKS

BARITONE GUITAR METHOD
00242055	Book/Online Audio	$12.99

GUITAR FOR KIDS
00865003	Method Book 1/Online Audio	$12.99
00697402	Songbook/Online Audio	$9.99
00128437	Method Book 2/Online Audio	$12.99

MUSIC THEORY FOR GUITARISTS
00695790	Book/Online Audio	$19.99

TENOR GUITAR METHOD
00148330	Book/Online Audio	$12.99

12-STRING GUITAR METHOD
00249528	Book/Online Audio	$19.99

METHOD SUPPLEMENTS

ARPEGGIO FINDER
00697352	6" x 9" Edition	$6.99
00697351	9" x 12" Edition	$9.99

BARRE CHORDS
00697406	Book/Online Audio	$14.99

CHORD, SCALE & ARPEGGIO FINDER
00697410	Book Only	$19.99

GUITAR TECHNIQUES
00697389	Book/Online Audio	$16.99

INCREDIBLE CHORD FINDER
00697200	6" x 9" Edition	$7.99
00697208	9" x 12" Edition	$7.99

INCREDIBLE SCALE FINDER
00695568	6" x 9" Edition	$9.99
00695490	9" x 12" Edition	$9.99

LEAD LICKS
00697345	Book/Online Audio	$10.99

RHYTHM RIFFS
00697346	Book/Online Audio	$14.99

SONGBOOKS

CLASSICAL GUITAR PIECES
00697388	Book/Online Audio	$9.99

EASY POP MELODIES
00697281	Book Only	$7.99
00697440	Book/Online Audio	$14.99

(MORE) EASY POP MELODIES
00697280	Book Only	$6.99
00697269	Book/Online Audio	$14.99

(EVEN MORE) EASY POP MELODIES
00699154	Book Only	$6.99
00697439	Book/Online Audio	$14.99

EASY POP RHYTHMS
00697336	Book Only	$7.99
00697441	Book/Online Audio	$14.99

(MORE) EASY POP RHYTHMS
00697338	Book Only	$7.99
00697322	Book/Online Audio	$14.99

(EVEN MORE) EASY POP RHYTHMS
00697340	Book Only	$7.99
00697323	Book/Online Audio	$14.99

EASY POP CHRISTMAS MELODIES
00697417	Book Only	$9.99
00697416	Book/Online Audio	$14.99

EASY POP CHRISTMAS RHYTHMS
00278177	Book Only	$6.99
00278175	Book/Online Audio	$14.99

EASY SOLO GUITAR PIECES
00110407	Book Only	$9.99

REFERENCE

GUITAR PRACTICE PLANNER
00697401	Book Only	$5.99

GUITAR SETUP & MAINTENANCE
00697427	6" x 9" Edition	$14.99
00697421	9" x 12" Edition	$12.99

For more info, songlists, or to purchase these and more books from your favorite music retailer, go to

halleonard.com